Mrs Warren's Profession

George Bernard Shaw

ACT I

[Summer afternoon in a cottage garden on the eastern slope of a hill a little south of Haslemere in Surrey. Looking up the hill, the cottage is seen in the left hand corner of the garden, with its thatched roof and porch, and a large latticed window to the left of the porch. A paling completely shuts in the garden, except for a gate on the right. The common rises uphill beyond the paling to the sky line. Some folded canvas garden chairs are leaning against the side bench in the porch. A lady's bicycle is propped against the wall, under the window. A little to the right of the porch a hammock is slung from two posts. A big canvas umbrella, stuck in the ground, keeps the sun off the hammock, in which a young lady is reading and making notes, her head towards the cottage and her feet towards the gate. In front of the hammock, and within reach of her hand, is a common kitchen chair, with a pile of serious-looking books and a supply of writing paper on it.]

[A gentleman walking on the common comes into sight from behind the cottage. He is hardly past middle age, with something of the artist about him, unconventionally but carefully dressed, and clean-shaven except for a moustache, with an eager susceptible face and very amiable and considerate manners. He has silky black hair, with waves of grey and white in it. His eyebrows are white, his moustache black. He seems not certain of his way. He looks over the palings; takes stock of the place; and sees the young lady.]

THE GENTLEMAN [taking off his hat] I beg your pardon. Can you direct me to Hindhead View--Mrs Alison's?

THE YOUNG LADY [glancing up from her book] This is Mrs Alison's. [She resumes her work].

THE GENTLEMAN. Indeed! Perhaps--may I ask are you Miss Vivie Warren?

THE YOUNG LADY [sharply, as she turns on her elbow to get a good look at him] Yes.

THE GENTLEMAN [daunted and conciliatory] I'm afraid I appear intrusive. My name is Praed. [Vivie at once throws her books upon the chair, and gets out of the hammock]. Oh, pray don't let me disturb you.

VIVIE [striding to the gate and opening it for him] Come in, Mr Praed. [He comes in]. Glad to see you. [She proffers her hand and takes his with a resolute and hearty grip. She is an attractive specimen of the sensible, able, highly-educated young middle-class Englishwoman. Age 22. Prompt, strong, confident, self-possessed. Plain business-like dress, but not dowdy. She wears a chatelaine at her belt, with a fountain pen and a paper knife among its pendants].

PRAED. Very kind of you indeed, Miss Warren. [She shuts the gate with a vigorous slam. He passes in to the middle of the garden, exercising his fingers, which are slightly numbed by her greeting]. Has your mother arrived?

VIVIE [quickly, evidently scenting aggression] Is she coming?

PRAED [surprised] Didn't you expect us?

VIVIE. No.

PRAED. Now, goodness me, I hope I've not mistaken the day. That would be just like me, you know. Your mother arranged that she was to come down from London and that I was to come over from Horsham to be introduced to you.

VIVIE [not at all pleased] Did she? Hm! My mother has rather a trick of taking me by surprise--to see how I behave myself while she's away, I suppose. I fancy I shall take my mother very much by surprise one of these days, if she makes arrangements that concern me without consulting me beforehand. She hasnt come.

PRAED [embarrassed] I'm really very sorry.

VIVIE [throwing off her displeasure] It's not your fault, Mr Praed, is it? And I'm very glad you've come. You are the only one of my mother's friends I have ever asked her to bring to see me.

PRAED [relieved and delighted] Oh, now this is really very good of you, Miss Warren!

VIVIE. Will you come indoors; or would you rather sit out here and talk?

PRAED. It will be nicer out here, don't you think?

VIVIE. Then I'll go and get you a chair. [She goes to the porch for a garden chair].

PRAED [following her] Oh, pray, pray! Allow me. [He lays hands on the chair].

VIVIE [letting him take it] Take care of your fingers; theyre rather dodgy things, those chairs. [She goes across to the chair with the books on it; pitches them into the hammock; and brings the chair forward with one swing].

PRAED [who has just unfolded his chair] Oh, now do let me take that hard chair. I like hard chairs.

VIVIE. So do I. Sit down, Mr Praed. [This invitation she gives with a genial peremptoriness, his anxiety to please her clearly striking her as a sign of weakness of character on his part. But he does not immediately obey].

PRAED. By the way, though, hadnt we better go to the station to meet your mother?

VIVIE [coolly] Why? She knows the way.

PRAED [disconcerted] Er--I suppose she does [he sits down].

VIVIE. Do you know, you are just like what I expected. I hope you are disposed to be friends with me.

PRAED [again beaming] Thank you, my *dear* Miss Warren; thank you. Dear me! I'm so glad your mother hasnt spoilt you!

VIVIE. How?

PRAED. Well, in making you too conventional. You know, my dear Miss Warren, I am a born anarchist. I hate authority. It spoils the relations between parent and child; even between mother and daughter. Now I was always afraid that your mother would strain her authority to make you very conventional. It's such a relief to find that she hasnt.

VIVIE. Oh! have I been behaving unconventionally?

PRAED. Oh no: oh dear no. At least, not conventionally unconventionally, you understand. [She nods and sits down. He goes on, with a cordial outburst] But it was so charming of you to say that you were disposed to be friends with me! You modern young ladies are splendid: perfectly splendid!

VIVIE [dubiously] Eh? [watching him with dawning disappointment as to the quality of his brains and character].

PRAED. When I was your age, young men and women were afraid of each other: there was no good fellowship. Nothing real. Only gallantry copied out of novels, and as vulgar and affected as it could be. Maidenly reserve! gentlemanly chivalry! always saying no when you meant yes! simple purgatory for shy and sincere souls.

VIVIE. Yes, I imagine there must have been a frightful waste of time. Especially women's time.

PRAED. Oh, waste of life, waste of everything. But things are improving. Do you know, I have been in a positive state of excitement about meeting you ever since your magnificent achievements at Cambridge: a thing unheard of in my day. It was perfectly splendid, your tieing with the third wrangler. Just the right place, you know. The first wrangler is always a dreamy, morbid fellow, in whom the thing is pushed to the length of a disease.

VIVIE. It doesn't pay. I wouldn't do it again for the same money.

PRAED [aghast] The same money!

VIVIE. Yes. Fifty pounds. Perhaps you don't know how it was. Mrs Latham, my tutor at Newnham, told my mother that I could distinguish myself in the mathematical tripos if I went in for it in earnest. The papers were full just then of Phillipa Summers beating the senior wrangler. You remember about it, of course.

PRAED [shakes his head energetically] !!!

VIVIE. Well, anyhow, she did; and nothing would please my mother but that I should do the same thing. I said flatly that it was not worth my while to face the grind since I was not going in for teaching; but I offered to try for fourth wrangler or thereabouts for fifty pounds. She closed with me at that, after a little grumbling; and I was better than my bargain.

But I wouldn't do it again for that. Two hundred pounds would have been nearer the mark.

PRAED [much damped] Lord bless me! Thats a very practical way of looking at it.

VIVIE. Did you expect to find me an unpractical person?

PRAED. But surely it's practical to consider not only the work these honors cost, but also the culture they bring.

VIVIE. Culture! My dear Mr Praed: do you know what the mathematical tripos means? It means grind, grind, grind for six to eight hours a day at mathematics, and nothing but mathematics.

I'm supposed to know something about science; but I know nothing except the mathematics it involves. I can make calculations for engineers, electricians, insurance companies, and so on; but I know next to nothing about engineering or electricity or insurance. I don't even know arithmetic well. Outside mathematics, lawn-tennis, eating, sleeping, cycling, and walking, I'm a more ignorant barbarian than any woman could possibly be who hadn't gone in for the tripos.

PRAED [revolted] What a monstrous, wicked, rascally system! I knew it! I felt at once that it meant destroying all that makes womanhood beautiful!

VIVIE. I don't object to it on that score in the least. I shall turn it to very good account, I assure you.

PRAED. Pooh! In what way?

VIVIE. I shall set up chambers in the City, and work at actuarial calculations and conveyancing. Under cover of that I shall do some law, with one eye on the Stock Exchange all the time. I've come down here by myself to read law: not for a holiday, as my mother imagines. I hate holidays.

PRAED. You make my blood run cold. Are you to have no romance, no beauty in your life?

VIVIE. I don't care for either, I assure you.

PRAED. You can't mean that.

VIVIE. Oh yes I do. I like working and getting paid for it. When I'm tired of working, I like a comfortable chair, a cigar, a little whisky, and a novel with a good detective story in it.

PRAED [rising in a frenzy of repudiation] I don't believe it. I am an artist; and I can't believe it: I refuse to believe it. It's only that you havn't discovered yet what a wonderful world art can open up to you.

VIVIE. Yes I have. Last May I spent six weeks in London with Honoria Fraser. Mamma thought we were doing a round of sightseeing together; but I was really at Honoria's chambers in Chancery Lane every day, working away at actuarial calculations for her, and helping her as well as a greenhorn could. In the evenings we smoked and talked, and never dreamt of going out except for exercise. And I never enjoyed myself more in my life.

I cleared all my expenses and got initiated into the business without a fee in the bargain.

PRAED. But bless my heart and soul, Miss Warren, do you call that discovering art?

VIVIE. Wait a bit. That wasn't the beginning. I went up to town on an invitation from some artistic people in Fitzjohn's Avenue: one of the girls was a Newnham chum. They took me to the National Gallery--

PRAED [approving] Ah!! [He sits down, much relieved].

VIVIE [continuing]--to the Opera--

PRAED [still more pleased] Good!

VIVIE.--and to a concert where the band played all the evening: Beethoven and Wagner and so on. I wouldn't go through that experience again for anything you could offer me. I held out for civility's sake until the third day; and then I said, plump out, that I couldn't stand any more of it, and went off to Chancery Lane. N o w you know the sort of perfectly splendid modern young lady I am. How do you think I shall get on with my mother?

PRAED [startled] Well, I hope--er--

VIVIE. It's not so much what you hope as what you believe, that I want to know.

PRAED. Well, frankly, I am afraid your mother will be a little disappointed. Not from any shortcoming on your part, you know: I don't mean that. But you are so different from her ideal.

VIVIE. Her what?!

PRAED. Her ideal.

VIVIE. Do you mean her ideal of ME?

PRAED. Yes.

VIVIE. What on earth is it like?

PRAED. Well, you must have observed, Miss Warren, that people who are dissatisfied with their own bringing-up generally think that the world would be all right if everybody were to be brought up quite differently. Now your mother's life has been--er--I suppose you know--

VIVIE. Don't suppose anything, Mr Praed. I hardly know my mother. Since I was a child I have lived in England, at school or at college, or with people paid to take charge of me. I have been boarded out all my life. My mother has lived in Brussels or Vienna and never let me go to her. I only see her when she visits England for a few days. I don't complain: it's been very pleasant; for people have been very good to me; and there has always been plenty of money to make things smooth. But don't imagine I know anything about my mother. I know far less than you do.

PRAED [very ill at ease] In that case--[He stops, quite at a loss. Then, with a forced attempt at gaiety] But what nonsense we are talking! Of course you and your mother will get on capitally. [He rises, and looks abroad at the view]. What a charming little place you have here!

VIVIE [unmoved] Rather a violent change of subject, Mr Praed. Why won't my mother's life bear being talked about?

PRAED. Oh, you mustn't say that. Isn't it natural that I should have a certain delicacy in talking to my old friend's daughter about her behind her back? You and she will have plenty of opportunity of talking about it when she comes.

VIVIE. No: she won't talk about it either. [Rising] However, I daresay you have good reasons for telling me nothing. Only, mind this, Mr Praed,

I expect there will be a battle royal when my mother hears of my Chancery Lane project.

PRAED [ruefully] I'm afraid there will.

VIVIE. Well, I shall win because I want nothing but my fare to London to start there to-morrow earning my own living by devilling for Honoria. Besides, I have no mysteries to keep up; and it seems she has. I shall use that advantage over her if necessary.

PRAED [greatly shocked] Oh no! No, pray. Youd not do such a thing.

VIVIE. Then tell me why not.

PRAED. I really cannot. I appeal to your good feeling. [She smiles at his sentimentality]. Besides, you may be too bold. Your mother is not to be trifled with when she's angry.

VIVIE. You can't frighten me, Mr Praed. In that month at Chancery Lane I had opportunities of taking the measure of one or two women v e r y like my mother. You may back me to win. But if I hit harder in my ignorance than I need, remember it is you who refuse to enlighten me. Now, let us drop the subject. [She takes her chair and replaces it near the hammock with the same vigorous swing as before].

PRAED [taking a desperate resolution] One word, Miss Warren. I had better tell you. It's very difficult; but--

[Mrs Warren and Sir George Crofts arrive at the gate. Mrs Warren is between 40 and 50, formerly pretty, showily dressed in a brilliant hat and a gay blouse fitting tightly over her bust and flanked by fashionable sleeves. Rather spoilt and domineering, and decidedly vulgar, but, on the whole, a genial and fairly presentable old blackguard of a woman.]

[Crofts is a tall powerfully-built man of about 50, fashionably dressed in the style of a young man. Nasal voice, reedier than might be expected from his strong frame. Clean-shaven bulldog jaws, large flat ears, and thick neck: gentlemanly combination of the most brutal types of city man, sporting man, and man about town.]

VIVIE. Here they are. [Coming to them as they enter the garden] How do, mater? Mr Praed's been here this half hour, waiting for you.

MRS WARREN. Well, if you've been waiting, Praddy, it's your own fault: I thought youd have had the gumption to know I was coming by the 3.10 train. Vivie: put your hat on, dear: youll get sunburnt. Oh, I forgot to introduce you. Sir George Crofts: my little Vivie.

[Crofts advances to Vivie with his most courtly manner. She nods, but makes no motion to shake hands.]

CROFTS. May I shake hands with a young lady whom I have known by reputation very long as the daughter of one of my oldest friends?

VIVIE [who has been looking him up and down sharply] If you like.

[She takes his tenderly proferred hand and gives it a squeeze that makes him open his eyes; then turns away, and says to her mother] Will you come in, or shall I get a couple more chairs? [She goes into the porch for the chairs].

MRS WARREN. Well, George, what do you think of her?

CROFTS [ruefully] She has a powerful fist. Did you shake hands with her, Praed?

PRAED. Yes: it will pass off presently.

CROFTS. I hope so. [Vivie reappears with two more chairs. He hurries to her assistance]. Allow me.

MRS WARREN [patronizingly] Let Sir George help you with the chairs, dear.

VIVIE [pitching them into his arms] Here you are. [She dusts her hands and turns to Mrs Warren]. Youd like some tea, wouldn't you?

MRS WARREN [sitting in Praed's chair and fanning herself] I'm dying for a drop to drink.

VIVIE. I'll see about it. [She goes into the cottage].

[Sir George has by this time managed to unfold a chair and plant it by Mrs Warren, on her left. He throws the other on the grass and sits down, looking dejected and rather foolish, with the handle of his stick in his mouth. Praed, still very uneasy, fidgets around the garden on their right.]

MRS WARREN [to Praed, looking at Crofts] Just look at him, Praddy: he looks cheerful, don't he? He's been worrying my life out these three years to have that little girl of mine shewn to him; and now that Ive done it, he's quite out of countenance. [Briskly] Come! sit up, George; and take your stick out of your mouth. [Crofts sulkily obeys].

PRAED. I think, you know--if you don't mind my saying so--that we had better get out of the habit of thinking of her as a little girl. You see she has really distinguished herself; and I'm not sure, from what I have seen of her, that she is not older than any of us.

MRS WARREN [greatly amused] Only listen to him, George! Older than any of us! Well she *has* been stuffing you nicely with her importance.

PRAED. But young people are particularly sensitive about being treated in that way.

MRS WARREN. Yes; and young people have to get all that nonsense taken out of them, and good deal more besides. Don't you interfere, Praddy: I know how to treat my own child as well as you do. [Praed, with a grave shake of his head, walks up the garden with his hands behind his back. Mrs Warren pretends to laugh, but looks after him with perceptible concern. Then, she whispers to Crofts] Whats the matter with him? What does he take it like that for?

CROFTS [morosely] Youre afraid of Praed.

MRS WARREN. What! Me! Afraid of dear old Praddy! Why, a fly wouldn't be afraid of him.

CROFTS. *You're* afraid of him.

MRS WARREN [angry] I'll trouble you to mind your own business, and not try any of your sulks on me. I'm not afraid of y o u, anyhow. If you can't make yourself agreeable, youd better go home. [She gets up, and, turning her back on him, finds herself face to face with Praed]. Come, Praddy, I know it was only your tender-heartedness. Youre afraid I'll bully her.

PRAED. My dear Kitty: you think I'm offended. Don't imagine that: pray don't. But you know I often notice things that escape you; and though you never take my advice, you sometimes admit afterwards that you ought to have taken it.

MRS WARREN. Well, what do you notice now?

PRAED. Only that Vivie is a grown woman. Pray, Kitty, treat her with every respect.

MRS WARREN [with genuine amazement] Respect! Treat my own daughter with respect! What next, pray!

VIVIE [appearing at the cottage door and calling to Mrs Warren] Mother: will you come to my room before tea?

MRS WARREN. Yes, dearie. [She laughs indulgently at Praed's gravity, and pats him on the cheek as she passes him on her way to the porch]. Don't be cross, Praddy. [She follows Vivie into the cottage].

CROFTS [furtively] I say, Praed.

PRAED. Yes.

CROFTS. I want to ask you a rather particular question.

PRAED. Certainly. [He takes Mrs Warren's chair and sits close to Crofts].

CROFTS. Thats right: they might hear us from the window. Look here: did Kitty every tell you who that girl's father is?

PRAED. Never.

CROFTS. Have you any suspicion of who it might be?

PRAED. None.

CROFTS [not believing him] I know, of course, that you perhaps might feel bound not to tell if she had said anything to you. But it's very awkward to be uncertain about it now that we shall be meeting the girl every day. We don't exactly know how we ought to feel towards her.

PRAED. What difference can that make? We take her on her own merits. What does it matter who her father was?

CROFTS [suspiciously] Then you know who he was?

PRAED [with a touch of temper] I said no just now. Did you not hear me?

CROFTS. Look here, Praed. I ask you as a particular favor. If you do know [movement of protest from Praed]--I only say, if you know, you might at least set my mind at rest about her. The fact is, I fell attracted.

PRAED [sternly] What do you mean?

CROFTS. Oh, don't be alarmed: it's quite an innocent feeling. Thats what puzzles me about it. Why, for all I know, *I* might be her father.

PRAED. You! Impossible!

CROFTS [catching him up cunningly] You know for certain that I'm not?

PRAED. I know nothing about it, I tell you, any more than you. But really, Crofts--oh no, it's out of the question. Theres not the least resemblance.

CROFTS. As to that, theres no resemblance between her and her mother that I can see. I suppose she's not y o u r daughter, is she?

PRAED [rising indignantly] Really, Crofts--!

CROFTS. No offence, Praed. Quite allowable as between two men of the world.

PRAED [recovering himself with an effort and speaking gently and gravely] Now listen to me, my dear Crofts. [He sits down again].

I have nothing to do with that side of Mrs Warren's life, and never had. She has never spoken to me about it; and of course I have never spoken to her about it. Your delicacy will tell you that a handsome woman needs some friends who are not--well, not on that footing with her. The effect of her own beauty would become a torment to her if she could not escape from it occasionally. You are probably on much more confidential terms with Kitty than I am. Surely you can ask her the question yourself.

CROFTS. I h a v e asked her, often enough. But she's so determined to keep the child all to herself that she would deny that it ever had a father if she could. [Rising] I'm thoroughly uncomfortable about it, Praed.

PRAED [rising also] Well, as you are, at all events, old enough to be her father, I don't mind agreeing that we both regard Miss Vivie in a parental way, as a young girl who we are bound to protect and help. What do you say?

CROFTS [aggressively] I'm no older than you, if you come to that.

PRAED. Yes you are, my dear fellow: you were born old. I was born a boy: Ive never been able to feel the assurance of a grown-up man in my life. [He folds his chair and carries it to the porch].

MRS WARREN [calling from within the cottage] Prad-dee! George! Tea-ea-ea-ea!

CROFTS [hastily] She's calling us. [He hurries in].

[Praed shakes his head bodingly, and is following Crofts when he is hailed by a young gentleman who has just appeared on the common, and is making for the gate. He is pleasant, pretty, smartly dressed, cleverly good-for-nothing, not long turned 20, with a charming voice and agreeably disrespectful manners. He carries a light sporting magazine rifle.]

THE YOUNG GENTLEMAN. Hallo! Praed!

PRAED. Why, Frank Gardner! [Frank comes in and shakes hands cordially]. What on earth are you doing here?

FRANK. Staying with my father.

PRAED. The Roman father?

FRANK. He's rector here. I'm living with my people this autumn for the sake of economy. Things came to a crisis in July: the Roman father had to pay my debts. He's stony broke in consequence; and so am I. What are you up to in these parts? do you know the people here?

PRAED. Yes: I'm spending the day with a Miss Warren.

FRANK [enthusiastically] What! Do you know Vivie? Isn't she a jolly girl? I'm teaching her to shoot with this [putting down the rifle]. I'm so glad she knows you: youre just the sort of fellow she ought to know. [He smiles, and raises the charming voice almost to a singing tone as he exclaims] It's e v e r so jolly to find you here, Praed.

PRAED. I'm an old friend of her mother. Mrs Warren brought me over to make her daughter's acquaintance.

FRANK. The mother! Is *she* here?

PRAED. Yes: inside, at tea.

MRS WARREN [calling from within] Prad-dee-ee-ee-eee! The tea-cake'll be cold.

xiv

PRAED [calling] Yes, Mrs Warren. In a moment. I've just met a friend here.

MRS WARREN. A what?

PRAED [louder] A friend.

MRS WARREN. Bring him in.

PRAED. All right. [To Frank] Will you accept the invitation?

FRANK [incredulous, but immensely amused] Is that Vivie's mother?

PRAED. Yes.

FRANK. By Jove! What a lark! Do you think she'll like me?

PRAED. I've no doubt youll make yourself popular, as usual. Come in and try [moving towards the house].

FRANK. Stop a bit. [Seriously] I want to take you into my confidence.

PRAED. Pray don't. It's only some fresh folly, like the barmaid at Redhill.

FRANK. It's ever so much more serious than that. You say you've only just met Vivie for the first time?

PRAED. Yes.

FRANK [rhapsodically] Then you can have no idea what a girl she is. Such character! Such sense! And her cleverness! Oh, my eye, Praed, but I can tell you she is clever! And--need I add?--she loves me.

CROFTS [putting his head out of the window] I say, Praed: what are you about? Do come along. [He disappears].

FRANK. Hallo! Sort of chap that would take a prize at a dog show, ain't he? Who's he?

PRAED. Sir George Crofts, an old friend of Mrs Warren's. I think we had better come in.

[On their way to the porch they are interrupted by a call from the gate. Turning, they see an elderly clergyman looking over it.]

THE CLERGYMAN [calling] Frank!

FRANK. Hallo! [To Praed] The Roman father. [To the clergyman] Yes, gov'nor: all right: presently. [To Praed] Look here, Praed: youd better go in to tea. I'll join you directly.

PRAED. Very good. [He goes into the cottage].

[The clergyman remains outside the gate, with his hands on the top of it. The Rev. Samuel Gardner, a beneficed clergyman of the Established Church, is over 50. Externally he is pretentious, booming, noisy, important. Really he is that obsolescent phenomenon the fool of the family dumped on the Church by his father the patron, clamorously asserting himself as father and clergyman without being able to command respect in either capacity.]

REV. S. Well, sir. Who are your friends here, if I may ask?

FRANK. Oh, it's all right, gov'nor! Come in.

REV. S. No, sir; not until I know whose garden I am entering.

FRANK. It's all right. It's Miss Warren's.

REV. S. I have not seen her at church since she came.

FRANK. Of course not: she's a third wrangler. Ever so intellectual. Took a higher degree than you did; so why should she go to hear you preach?

REV. S. Don't be disrespectful, sir.

FRANK. Oh, it don't matter: nobody hears us. Come in. [He opens the gate, unceremoniously pulling his father with it into the garden]. I want to introduce you to her. Do you remember the advice you gave me last July, gov'nor?

REV. S. [severely] Yes. I advised you to conquer your idleness and flippancy, and to work your way into an honorable profession and live on it and not upon me.

FRANK. No: thats what you thought of afterwards. What you actually said was that since I had neither brains nor money, I'd better turn my good looks to account by marrying someone with both. Well, look here. Miss Warren has brains: you can't deny that.

REV. S. Brains are not everything.

FRANK. No, of course not: theres the money--

REV. S. [interrupting him austerely] I was not thinking of money, sir. I was speaking of higher things. Social position, for instance.

FRANK. I don't care a rap about that.

REV. S. But I do, sir.

FRANK. Well, nobody wants y o u to marry her. Anyhow, she has what amounts to a high Cambridge degree; and she seems to have as much money as she wants.

REV. S. [sinking into a feeble vein of humor] I greatly doubt whether she has as much money as y o u will want.

FRANK. Oh, come: I havn't been so very extravagant. I live ever so quietly; I don't drink; I don't bet much; and I never go regularly to the razzle-dazzle as you did when you were my age.

REV. S. [booming hollowly] Silence, sir.

FRANK. Well, you told me yourself, when I was making every such an ass of myself about the barmaid at Redhill, that you once offered a woman fifty pounds for the letters you wrote to her when--

REV. S. [terrified] Sh-sh-sh, Frank, for Heaven's sake! [He looks round apprehensively Seeing no one within earshot he plucks up courage to boom again, but more subduedly]. You are taking an ungentlemanly advantage of what I confided to you for your own good, to save you from an error you would have repented all your life long. Take warning by your father's follies, sir; and don't make them an excuse for your own.

FRANK. Did you ever hear the story of the Duke of Wellington and his letters?

REV. S. No, sir; and I don't want to hear it.

FRANK. The old Iron Duke didn't throw away fifty pounds: not he. He just wrote: "Dear Jenny: publish and be damned! Yours affectionately, Wellington." Thats what you should have done.

REV. S. [piteously] Frank, my boy: when I wrote those letters I put myself into that woman's power. When I told you about them I put myself, to some extent, I am sorry to say, in your power. She refused my money with these words, which I shall never forget. "Knowledge is power" she said; "and I never sell power."

Thats more than twenty years ago; and she has never made use of her power or caused me a moment's uneasiness. You are behaving worse to me than she did, Frank.

FRANK. Oh yes I dare say! Did you ever preach at her the way you preach at me every day?

REV. S. [wounded almost to tears] I leave you, sir. You are incorrigible. [He turns towards the gate].

FRANK [utterly unmoved] Tell them I shan't be home to tea, will you, gov'nor, like a good fellow? [He moves towards the cottage door and is met by Praed and Vivie coming out].

VIVIE [to Frank] Is that your father, Frank? I do so want to meet him.

FRANK. Certainly. [Calling after his father] Gov'nor. Youre wanted. [The parson turns at the gate, fumbling nervously at his hat. Praed crosses the garden to the opposite side, beaming in anticipation of civilities]. My father: Miss Warren.

VIVIE [going to the clergyman and shaking his hand] Very glad to see you here, Mr Gardner. [Calling to the cottage] Mother: come along: youre wanted.

[Mrs Warren appears on the threshold, and is immediately transfixed, recognizing the clergyman.]

VIVIE [continuing] Let me introduce--

MRS WARREN [swooping on the Reverend Samuel] Why it's Sam Gardner, gone into the Church! Well, I never! Don't you know us, Sam? This is George Crofts, as large as life and twice as natural. Don't you remember me?

REV. S. [very red] I really--er--

MRS WARREN. Of course you do. Why, I have a whole album of your letters still: I came across them only the other day.

REV. S. [miserably confused] Miss Vavasour, I believe.

MRS WARREN [correcting him quickly in a loud whisper] Tch! Nonsense! Mrs Warren: don't you see my daughter there?

ACT II

[Inside the cottage after nightfall. Looking eastward from within instead of westward from without, the latticed window, with its curtains drawn, is now seen in the middle of the front wall of the cottage, with the porch door to the left of it. In the left-hand side wall is the door leading to the kitchen. Farther back against the same wall is a dresser with a candle and matches on it, and Frank's rifle standing beside them, with the barrel resting in the plate-rack. In the centre a table stands with a lighted lamp on it. Vivie's books and writing materials are on a table to the right of the window, against the wall. The fireplace is on the right, with a settle: there is no fire. Two of the chairs are set right and left of the table.]

[The cottage door opens, shewing a fine starlit night without; and Mrs Warren, her shoulders wrapped in a shawl borrowed from Vivie, enters, followed by Frank, who throws his cap on the window seat. She has had enough of walking, and gives a gasp of relief as she unpins her hat; takes it off; sticks the pin through the crown; and puts it on the table.]

MRS WARREN. O Lord! I don't know which is the worst of the country, the walking or the sitting at home with nothing to do. I could do with a whisky and soda now very well, if only they had such a things in this place.

FRANK. Perhaps Vivie's got some.

MRS WARREN. Nonsense! What would a young girl like her be doing with such things! Never mind: it don't matter. I wonder how she passes her time here! I'd a good deal rather be in Vienna.

FRANK. Let me take you there. [He helps her to take off her shawl, gallantly giving her shoulders a very perceptible squeeze as he does so].

MRS WARREN. Ah! would you? I'm beginning to think youre a chip of the old block.

FRANK. Like the gov'nor, eh? [He hangs the shawl on the nearest chair, and sits down].

MRS WARREN. Never you mind. What do you know about such things?

Youre only a boy. [She goes to the hearth to be farther from temptation].

FRANK. Do come to Vienna with me? It'd be ever such larks.

MRS WARREN. No, thank you. Vienna is no place for you--at least not until youre a little older. [She nods at him to emphasize this piece of advice. He makes a mock-piteous face, belied by his laughing eyes. She looks at him; then comes back to him]. Now, look here, little boy [taking his face in her hands and turning it up to her]: I know you through and through by your likeness to your father, better than you know yourself. Don't you go taking any silly ideas into your head about me. Do you hear?

FRANK [gallantly wooing her with his voice] Can't help it, my dear Mrs Warren: it runs in the family.

[She pretends to box his ears; then looks at the pretty laughing upturned face of a moment, tempted. At last she kisses him, and immediately turns away, out of patience with herself.]

MRS WARREN. There! I shouldn't have done that. I *am* wicked. Never you mind, my dear: it's only a motherly kiss. Go and make love to Vivie.

FRANK. So I have.

MRS WARREN [turning on him with a sharp note of alarm in her voice] What!

FRANK. Vivie and I are ever such chums.

MRS WARREN. What do you mean? Now see here: I won't have any young scamp tampering with my little girl. Do you hear? I won't have it.

FRANK [quite unabashed] My dear Mrs Warren: don't you be alarmed. My intentions are honorable: ever so honorable; and your little girl is jolly well able to take care of herself. She don't need looking after half so much as her mother. She ain't so handsome, you know.

MRS WARREN [taken aback by his assurance] Well, you have got a nice healthy two inches of cheek all over you. I don't know where you got it. Not from your father, anyhow.

CROFTS [in the garden] The gipsies, I suppose?

REV. S. [replying] The broomsquires are far worse.

MRS WARREN [to Frank] S-sh! Remember! you've had your warning.

[Crofts and the Reverend Samuel Gardner come in from the garden, the clergyman continuing his conversation as he enters.]

REV. S. The perjury at the Winchester assizes is deplorable.

MRS WARREN. Well? what became of you two? And wheres Praddy and Vivie?

CROFTS [putting his hat on the settle and his stick in the chimney corner] They went up the hill. We went to the village. I wanted a drink. [He sits down on the settle, putting his legs up along the seat].

MRS WARREN. Well, she oughtn't to go off like that without telling me. [To Frank] Get your father a chair, Frank: where are your manners? [Frank springs up and gracefully offers his father his chair; then takes another from the wall and sits down at the table, in the middle, with his father on his right and Mrs Warren on his left]. George: where are you going to stay to-night? You can't stay here. And whats Praddy going to do?

CROFTS. Gardner'll put me up.

MRS WARREN. Oh, no doubt you've taken care of yourself! But what about Praddy?

CROFTS. Don't know. I suppose he can sleep at the inn.

MRS WARREN. Havn't you room for him, Sam?

REV. S. Well--er--you see, as rector here, I am not free to do as I like. Er--what is Mr Praed's social position?

MRS WARREN. Oh, he's all right: he's an architect. What an old stick-in-the-mud you are, Sam!

FRANK. Yes, it's all right, gov'nor. He built that place down in Wales for the Duke. Caernarvon Castle they call it. You must have heard of it. [He winks with lightning smartness at Mrs Warren, and regards his father blandly].

REV. S. Oh, in that case, of course we shall only be too happy. I suppose he knows the Duke personally.

FRANK. Oh, ever so intimately! We can stick him in Georgina's old room.

MRS WARREN. Well, thats settled. Now if those two would only come in and let us have supper. Theyve no right to stay out after dark like this.

CROFTS [aggressively] What harm are they doing you?

MRS WARREN. Well, harm or not, I don't like it.

FRANK. Better not wait for them, Mrs Warren. Praed will stay out as long as possible. He has never known before what it is to stray over the heath on a summer night with my Vivie.

CROFTS [sitting up in some consternation] I say, you know! Come!

REV. S. [rising, startled out of his professional manner into real force and sincerity] Frank, once and for all, it's out of the question. Mrs Warren will tell you that it's not to be thought of.

CROFTS. Of course not.

FRANK [with enchanting placidity] Is that so, Mrs Warren?

MRS WARREN [reflectively] Well, Sam, I don't know. If the girl wants to get married, no good can come of keeping her unmarried.

REV. S. [astounded] But married to *him!*--your daughter to my son! Only think: it's impossible.

CROFTS. Of course it's impossible. Don't be a fool, Kitty.

MRS WARREN [nettled] Why not? Isn't my daughter good enough for your son?

REV. S. But surely, my dear Mrs Warren, you know the reasons--

MRS WARREN [defiantly] I know no reasons. If you know any, you can tell them to the lad, or to the girl, or to your congregation, if you like.

REV. S. [collapsing helplessly into his chair] You know very well that I couldn't tell anyone the reasons. But my boy will believe me when I tell him there a r e reasons.

FRANK. Quite right, Dad: he will. But has your boy's conduct ever been influenced by your reasons?

CROFTS. You can't marry her; and thats all about it. [He gets up and stands on the hearth, with his back to the fireplace, frowning determinedly].

MRS WARREN [turning on him sharply] What have you got to do with it, pray?

FRANK [with his prettiest lyrical cadence] Precisely what I was going to ask, myself, in my own graceful fashion.

CROFTS [to Mrs Warren] I suppose you don't want to marry the girl to a man younger than herself and without either a profession or twopence to keep her on. Ask Sam, if you don't believe me. [To the parson] How much more money are you going to give him?

REV. S. Not another penny. He has had his patrimony; and he spent the last of it in July. [Mrs Warren's face falls].

CROFTS [watching her] There! I told you. [He resumes his place on the settle and puts his legs on the seat again, as if the matter were finally disposed of].

FRANK [plaintively] This is ever so mercenary. Do you suppose Miss Warren's going to marry for money? If we love one another--

MRS WARREN. Thank you. Your love's a pretty cheap commodity, my lad. If you have no means of keeping a wife, that settles it; you can't have Vivie.

FRANK [much amused] What do y o u say, gov'nor, eh?

REV. S. I agree with Mrs Warren.

FRANK. And good old Crofts has already expressed his opinion.

CROFTS [turning angrily on his elbow] Look here: I want none of your cheek.

FRANK [pointedly] I'm e v e r so sorry to surprise you, Crofts; but you allowed yourself the liberty of speaking to me like a father a moment ago. One father is enough, thank you.

CROFTS [contemptuously] Yah! [He turns away again].

FRANK [rising] Mrs Warren: I cannot give my Vivie up, even for your sake.

MRS WARREN [muttering] Young scamp!

FRANK [continuing] And as you no doubt intend to hold out other prospects to her, I shall lose no time in placing my case before her. [They stare at him; and he begins to declaim gracefully] He either fears his fate too much, Or his deserts are small, That dares not put it to the touch, To gain or lose it all.

[The cottage doors open whilst he is reciting; and Vivie and Praed come in. He breaks off. Praed puts his hat on the dresser. There is an immediate improvement in the company's behavior. Crofts takes down his legs from the settle and pulls himself together as Praed joins him at the fireplace. Mrs Warren loses her ease of manner and takes refuge in querulousness.]

MRS WARREN. Wherever have you been, Vivie?

VIVIE [taking off her hat and throwing it carelessly on the table] On the hill.

MRS WARREN. Well, you shouldn't go off like that without letting me know. How could I tell what had become of you? And night coming on too!

VIVIE [going to the door of the kitchen and opening it, ignoring her mother] Now, about supper? [All rise except Mrs Warren] We shall be rather crowded in here, I'm afraid.

MRS WARREN. Did you hear what I said, Vivie?

VIVIE [quietly] Yes, mother. [Reverting to the supper difficulty] How many are we? [Counting] One, two, three, four, five, six. Well, two will have to wait until the rest are done: Mrs Alison has only plates and knives for four.

PRAED. Oh, it doesn't matter about me. I--

VIVIE. You have had a long walk and are hungry, Mr Praed: you shall have your supper at once. I can wait myself. I want one person to wait with me. Frank: are you hungry?

FRANK. Not the least in the world. Completely off my peck, in fact.

MRS WARREN [to Crofts] Neither are you, George. You can wait.

CROFTS. Oh, hang it, I've eaten nothing since tea-time. Can't Sam do it?

FRANK. Would you starve my poor father?

REV. S. [testily] Allow me to speak for myself, sir. I am perfectly willing to wait.

VIVIE [decisively] There's no need. Only two are wanted. [She opens the door of the kitchen]. Will you take my mother in, Mr Gardner. [The parson takes Mrs Warren; and they pass into the kitchen. Praed and Crofts follow. All except Praed clearly disapprove of the arrangement, but do not know how to resist it. Vivie stands at the door looking in at them]. Can you squeeze past to that corner, Mr Praed: it's rather a tight fit. Take care of your coat against the white-wash: that right. Now, are you all comfortable?

PRAED [within] Quite, thank you.

MRS WARREN [within] Leave the door open, dearie. [Vivie frowns; but Frank checks her with a gesture, and steals to the cottage door, which he softly sets wide open]. Oh Lor, what a draught! Youd better shut it, dear.

[Vivie shuts it with a slam, and then, noting with disgust that her mother's hat and shawl are lying about, takes them tidily to the window seat, whilst Frank noiselessly shuts the cottage door.]

FRANK [exulting] Aha! Got rid of em. Well, Vivvums: what do you think of my governor?

VIVIE [preoccupied and serious] I've hardly spoken to him. He doesn't strike me as a particularly able person.

FRANK. Well, you know, the old man is not altogether such a fool as he looks. You see, he was shoved into the Church, rather; and in trying to live up to it he makes a much bigger ass of himself than he really is. I don't dislike him as much as you might expect. He means well. How do you think youll get on with him?

VIVIE [rather grimly] I don't think my future life will be much concerned with him, or with any of that old circle of my mother's, except perhaps Praed. [She sits down on the settle] What do you think of my mother?

FRANK. Really and truly?

VIVIE. Yes, really and truly.

FRANK. Well, she's ever so jolly. But she's rather a caution, isn't she? And Crofts! Oh, my eye, Crofts! [He sits beside her].

VIVIE. What a lot, Frank!

FRANK. What a crew!

VIVIE [with intense contempt for them] If I thought that *I* was like that--that I was going to be a waster, shifting along from one meal to another with no purpose, and no character, and no grit in me, I'd open an artery and bleed to death without one moment's hesitation.

FRANK. Oh no, you wouldn't. Why should they take any grind when they can afford not to? I wish I had their luck. No: what I object to is their form. It isn't the thing: it's slovenly, ever so slovenly.

VIVIE. Do you think your form will be any better when youre as old as Crofts, if you don't work?

FRANK. Of course I do. Ever so much better. Vivvums mustn't lecture: her little boy's incorrigible. [He attempts to take her face caressingly in his hands].

VIVIE [striking his hands down sharply] Off with you: Vivvums is not in a humor for petting her little boy this evening. [She rises and comes forward to the other side of the room].

FRANK [following her] How unkind!

VIVIE [stamping at him] Be serious. I'm serious.

FRANK. Good. Let us talk learnedly, Miss Warren: do you know that all the most advanced thinkers are agreed that half the diseases of modern civilization are due to starvation of the affections of the young. Now, I--

VIVIE [cutting him short] You are very tiresome. [She opens the inner door] Have you room for Frank there? He's complaining of starvation.

MRS WARREN [within] Of course there is [clatter of knives and glasses as she moves the things on the table]. Here! theres room now beside me. Come along, Mr Frank.

FRANK. Her little boy will be ever so even with his Vivvums for this. [He passes into the kitchen].

MRS WARREN [within] Here, Vivie: come on you too, child. You must be famished. [She enters, followed by Crofts, who holds the door open with marked deference. She goes out without looking at him; and he shuts the door after her]. Why George, you can't be done: you've eaten nothing. Is there anything wrong with you?

CROFTS. Oh, all I wanted was a drink. [He thrusts his hands in his pockets, and begins prowling about the room, restless and sulky].

MRS WARREN. Well, I like enough to eat. But a little of that cold beef and cheese and lettuce goes a long way. [With a sigh of only half repletion she sits down lazily on the settle].

CROFTS. What do you go encouraging that young pup for?

MRS WARREN [on the alert at once] Now see here, George: what are you up to about that girl? I've been watching your way of looking at her. Remember: I know you and what your looks mean.

CROFTS. Theres no harm in looking at her, is there?

MRS WARREN. I'd put you out and pack you back to London pretty soon if I saw any of your nonsense. My girl's little finger is more to me than your whole body and soul. [Crofts receives this with a sneering grin. Mrs Warren, flushing a little at her failure to impose on him in the character of a theatrically devoted mother, adds in a lower key] Make your mind easy: the young pup has no more chance than you have.

CROFTS. Mayn't a man take an interest in a girl?

MRS WARREN. Not a man like you.

CROFTS. How old is she?

MRS WARREN. Never you mind how old she is.

CROFTS. Why do you make such a secret of it?

MRS WARREN. Because I choose.

CROFTS. Well, I'm not fifty yet; and my property is as good as it ever was--

MRS [interrupting him] Yes; because youre as stingy as youre vicious.

CROFTS [continuing] And a baronet isn't to be picked up every day. No other man in my position would put up with you for a mother-in-law. Why shouldn't she marry me?

MRS WARREN. You!

CROFTS. We three could live together quite comfortably. I'd die before her and leave her a bouncing widow with plenty of money. Why not? It's been growing in my mind all the time I've been walking with that fool inside there.

MRS WARREN [revolted] Yes; it's the sort of thing that *would* grow in your mind.

[He halts in his prowling; and the two look at one another, she steadfastly, with a sort of awe behind her contemptuous disgust: he stealthily, with a carnal gleam in his eye and a loose grin.]

CROFTS [suddenly becoming anxious and urgent as he sees no sign of sympathy in her] Look here, Kitty: youre a sensible woman: you needn't put on any moral airs. I'll ask no more questions; and you need answer none. I'll settle the whole property on her; and if you want a checque for yourself on the wedding day, you can name any figure you like--in reason.

MRS WARREN. So it's come to that with you, George, like all the other worn-out old creatures!

CROFTS [savagely] Damn you!

[Before she can retort the door of the kitchen is opened; and the voices of the others are heard returning. Crofts, unable to recover his presence of mind, hurries out of the cottage. The clergyman appears at the kitchen door.]

REV. S. [looking round] Where is Sir George?

MRS WARREN. Gone out to have a pipe. [The clergyman takes his hat from the table, and joins Mrs Warren at the fireside. Meanwhile, Vivie comes in, followed by Frank, who collapses into the nearest chair with an air of extreme exhaustion. Mrs Warren looks round at Vivie and says, with her affectation of maternal patronage even more forced than usual] Well, dearie: have you had a good supper?

VIVIE. You know what Mrs Alison's suppers are. [She turns to Frank and pets him] Poor Frank! was all the beef gone? did it get nothing but bread and cheese and ginger beer? [Seriously, as if she had done quite enough trifling for one evening] Her butter is really awful. I must get some down from the stores.

FRANK. Do, in Heaven's name!

[Vivie goes to the writing-table and makes a memorandum to order the butter. Praed comes in from the kitchen, putting up his handkerchief, which he has been using as a napkin.]

REV. S. Frank, my boy: it is time for us to be thinking of home.

Your mother does not know yet that we have visitors.

PRAED. I'm afraid we're giving trouble.

FRANK [rising] Not the least in the world: my mother will be delighted to see you. She's a genuinely intellectual artistic woman; and she sees nobody here from one year's end to another except the gov'nor; so you can imagine how jolly dull it pans out for her. [To his father] Y o u r e not intellectual or artistic: are you pater? So take Praed home at once; and I'll stay here and entertain Mrs Warren. Youll pick up Crofts in the garden. He'll be excellent company for the bull-pup.

PRAED [taking his hat from the dresser, and coming close to Frank] Come with us, Frank. Mrs Warren has not seen Miss Vivie for a long time; and we have prevented them from having a moment together yet.

FRANK [quite softened, and looking at Praed with romantic admiration] Of course. I forgot. Ever so thanks for reminding me. Perfect gentleman, Praddy. Always were. My ideal through life. [He rises to go, but pauses a moment between the two older men, and puts his hand on Praed's shoulder]. Ah, if you had only been my father instead of this unworthy old man! [He puts his other hand on his father's shoulder].

REV. S. [blustering] Silence, sir, silence: you are profane.

MRS WARREN [laughing heartily] You should keep him in better order, Sam. Good-night. Here: take George his hat and stick with my compliments.

REV. S. [taking them] Good-night. [They shake hands. As he passes Vivie he shakes hands with her also and bids her good-night. Then, in booming command, to Frank] Come along, sir, at once. [He goes out].

MRS WARREN. Byebye, Praddy.

PRAED. Byebye, Kitty.

[They shake hands affectionately and go out together, she accompanying him to the garden gate.]

FRANK [to Vivie] Kissums?

VIVIE [fiercely] No. I hate you. [She takes a couple of books and some paper from the writing-table, and sits down with them at the middle table, at the end next the fireplace].

FRANK [grimacing] Sorry. [He goes for his cap and rifle. Mrs Warren returns. He takes her hand] Good-night, dear Mrs Warren. [He kisses her hand. She snatches it away, her lips tightening, and looks more than half disposed to box his ears. He laughs mischievously and runs off, clapping-to the door behind him].

MRS WARREN [resigning herself to an evening of boredom now that the men are gone] Did you ever in your life hear anyone rattle on so? Isn't he a tease? [She sits at the table]. Now that I think of it, dearie, don't you go encouraging him. I'm sure he's a regular good-for-nothing.

VIVIE [rising to fetch more books] I'm afraid so. Poor Frank! I shall have to get rid of him; but I shall feel sorry for him, though he's not worth it. That man Crofts does not seem to me to be good for much either: is he? [She throws the books on the table rather roughly].

MRS WARREN [galled by Vivie's indifference] What do you know of men, child, to talk that way of them? Youll have to make up your mind to see a good deal of Sir George Crofts, as he's a friend of mine.

VIVIE [quite unmoved] Why? [She sits down and opens a book]. Do you expect that we shall be much together? You and I, I mean?

MRS WARREN [staring at her] Of course: until youre married. Youre not going back to college again.

VIVIE. Do you think my way of life would suit you? I doubt it.

MRS WARREN. Y o u r way of life! What do you mean?

VIVIE [cutting a page of her book with the paper knife on her chatelaine] Has it really never occurred to you, mother, that I have a way of life like other people?

MRS WARREN. What nonsense is this youre trying to talk? Do you want to shew your independence, now that youre a great little person at school? Don't be a fool, child.

VIVIE [indulgently] Thats all you have to say on the subject, is it, mother?

MRS WARREN [puzzled, then angry] Don't you keep on asking me questions like that. [Violently] Hold your tongue. [Vivie works on, losing no time, and saying nothing]. You and your way of life, indeed! What next? [She looks at Vivie again. No reply].

Your way of life will be what I please, so it will. [Another pause]. Ive been noticing these airs in you ever since you got that tripos or whatever you call it. If you think I'm going to put up with them, youre mistaken; and the sooner you find it out, the better. [Muttering] All I have to say on the subject, indeed! [Again raising her voice angrily] Do you know who youre speaking to, Miss?

VIVIE [looking across at her without raising her head from her book] No. Who are you? What are you?

MRS WARREN [rising breathless] You young imp!

VIVIE. Everybody knows my reputation, my social standing, and the profession I intend to pursue. I know nothing about you. What is that way of life which you invite me to share with you and Sir George Crofts, pray?

MRS WARREN. Take care. I shall do something I'll be sorry for after, and you too.

VIVIE [putting aside her books with cool decision] Well, let us drop the subject until you are better able to face it. [Looking critically at her mother] You want some good walks and a little lawn tennis to set you up. You are shockingly out of condition: you were not able to manage twenty yards uphill today without stopping to pant; and your wrists are mere rolls of fat. Look at mine. [She holds out her wrists].

MRS WARREN [after looking at her helplessly, begins to whimper] Vivie--

VIVIE [springing up sharply] Now pray don't begin to cry. Anything but that. I really cannot stand whimpering. I will go out of the room if you do.

MRS WARREN [piteously] Oh, my darling, how can you be so hard on me? Have I no rights over you as your mother?

VIVIE. A r e you my mother?

MRS WARREN. *Am* I your mother? Oh, Vivie!

VIVIE. Then where are our relatives? my father? our family friends? You claim the rights of a mother: the right to call me fool and child; to speak to me as no woman in authority over me at college dare speak to me; to dictate my way of life; and to force on me the acquaintance of a brute whom anyone can see to be the most vicious sort of London man about town. Before I give myself the trouble to resist such claims, I may as well find out whether they have any real existence.

MRS WARREN [distracted, throwing herself on her knees] Oh no, no.

Stop, stop. I *am* your mother: I swear it. Oh, you can't mean to turn on me--my own child! it's not natural. You believe me, don't you? Say you believe me.

VIVIE. Who was my father?

MRS WARREN. You don't know what youre asking. I can't tell you.

VIVIE [determinedly] Oh yes you can, if you like. I have a right to know; and you know very well that I have that right. You can refuse to tell me if you please; but if you do, you will see the last of me tomorrow morning.

MRS WARREN. Oh, it's too horrible to hear you talk like that. You wouldn't--you *couldn't* leave me.

VIVIE [ruthlessly] Yes, without a moment's hesitation, if you trifle with me about this. [Shivering with disgust] How can I feel sure that I may not have the contaminated blood of that brutal waster in my veins?

MRS WARREN. No, no. On my oath it's not he, nor any of the rest that you have ever met. I'm certain of that, at least.

[Vivie's eyes fasten sternly on her mother as the significance of this flashes on her.]

VIVIE [slowly] You are certain of that, at *least*. Ah! You mean that that is all you are certain of. [Thoughtfully] I see. [Mrs Warren buries her face in her hands]. Don't do that, mother: you know you don't feel it a bit. [Mrs Warren takes down her hands and looks up deplorably at Vivie, who takes out her watch and says] Well, that is enough for tonight. At what hour would you like breakfast? Is half-past eight too early for you?

MRS WARREN [wildly] My God, what sort of woman are you?

VIVIE [coolly] The sort the world is mostly made of, I should hope. Otherwise I don't understand how it gets its business done.

Come [taking her mother by the wrist and pulling her up pretty resolutely]: pull yourself together. Thats right.

MRS WARREN [querulously] Youre very rough with me, Vivie.

VIVIE. Nonsense. What about bed? It's past ten.

MRS WARREN [passionately] Whats the use of my going to bed? Do you think I could sleep?

VIVIE. Why not? I shall.

MRS WARREN. You! you've no heart. [She suddenly breaks out vehemently in her natural tongue--the dialect of a woman of the people--with all her affectations of maternal authority and conventional manners gone, and an overwhelming inspiration of true conviction and scorn in her] Oh, I wont bear it: I won't put up with the injustice of it. What right have you to set yourself up above me like this? You boast of what you are to me--to *me*, who gave you a chance of being what you are. What chance had I? Shame on you for a bad daughter and a stuck-up prude!

VIVIE [sitting down with a shrug, no longer confident; for her replies, which have sounded sensible and strong to her so far, now begin to ring rather woodenly and even priggishly against the new tone of her mother] Don't think for a moment I set myself above you in any way. You attacked me with the conventional authority of a mother: I defended myself with the conventional superiority of a respectable woman. Frankly, I am not going to stand any of your nonsense; and when you drop it I shall not expect you to stand any of mine. I shall always respect your right to your own opinions and your own way of life.

MRS WARREN. My own opinions and my own way of life! Listen to her talking! Do you think I was brought up like you? able to pick and choose my own way of life? Do you think I did what I did because I liked it, or thought it right, or wouldn't rather have gone to college and been a lady if I'd had the chance?

VIVIE. Everybody has some choice, mother. The poorest girl alive may not be able to choose between being Queen of England or Principal of Newnham; but she can choose between ragpicking and flowerselling, according to her taste. People are always blaming circumstances for what they are. I don't believe in circumstances. The people who get on in this world are the people who get up and look for the circumstances they want, and, if they can't find them, make them.

MRS WARREN. Oh, it's easy to talk, isn't it? Here! would you like to know what *my* circumstances were?

VIVIE. Yes: you had better tell me. Won't you sit down?

MRS WARREN. Oh, I'll sit down: don't you be afraid. [She plants her chair farther forward with brazen energy, and sits down. Vivie is impressed in spite of herself]. D'you know what your gran'mother was?

VIVIE. No.

MRS WARREN. No, you don't. I do. She called herself a widow and had a fried-fish shop down by the Mint, and kept herself and four daughters out of it. Two of us were sisters: that was me and Liz; and we were both good-looking and well made. I suppose our father was a well-fed man: mother pretended he was a gentleman; but I don't know. The other two were only half sisters: undersized, ugly, starved looking, hard working, honest poor creatures: Liz and I would have half-murdered them if mother hadn't half-murdered us to keep our hands off them. They were the respectable ones. Well, what did they get by their respectability? I'll tell you. One of them worked in a whitelead factory twelve hours a day for nine shillings a week until she died of lead poisoning. She only expected to get her hands a little paralyzed; but she died. The other was always held up to us as a model because she married a Government laborer in the Deptford victualling yard, and kept his room and the three children neat and tidy on eighteen shillings a week--until he took to drink. That was worth being respectable for, wasn't it?

VIVIE [now thoughtfully attentive] Did you and your sister think so?

MRS WARREN. Liz didn't, I can tell you: she had more spirit. We both went to a church school--that was part of the ladylike airs we gave ourselves to be superior to the children that knew nothing and went nowhere--and we stayed there until Liz went out one night and never came back. I know the schoolmistress thought I'd soon follow her example; for the clergyman was always warning me that Lizzie'd end by jumping off Waterloo Bridge. Poor fool: that was all he knew about it! But I was more afraid of the whitelead factory than I was of the river; and so would you have been in my place. That clergyman got me a situation as a scullery maid in a temperance restaurant where they sent out for anything you liked. Then I was a waitress; and then I went to the bar at Waterloo station: fourteen hours a day serving drinks and washing glasses for four shillings a week and my board. That was considered a great promotion for me. Well, one cold, wretched night, when I was so tired I could hardly keep myself awake, who should come up for a half of Scotch but Lizzie, in a long fur cloak, elegant and comfortable, with a lot of sovereigns in her purse.

VIVIE [grimly] My aunt Lizzie!

MRS WARREN. Yes; and a very good aunt to have, too. She's living down at Winchester now, close to the cathedral, one of the most respectable ladies there. Chaperones girls at the country ball, if you please. No river for Liz, thank you! You remind me of Liz a little: she was a first-rate business woman--saved money from the beginning--never let herself look too like what she was--never lost her head or threw away a chance. When she saw I'd grown up good-looking she said to me across the bar "What are you doing there, you little fool? wearing out your health and your appearance for other people's profit!" Liz was saving money then to take a house for herself in Brussels; and she thought we two could save faster than one. So she lent me some money and gave me a start; and I saved steadily and first paid her back, and then went into business with her as a partner. Why shouldn't I have done it? The house in Brussels was real high class: a much better place for a woman to be in than the factory where Anne Jane got poisoned. None of the girls were ever treated as I was treated in the scullery of that temperance place, or at the Waterloo bar, or at home. Would you have had me stay in them and become a worn out old drudge before I was forty?

VIVIE [intensely interested by this time] No; but why did you choose that business? Saving money and good management will succeed in any business.

MRS WARREN. Yes, saving money. But where can a woman get the money to save in any other business? Could y o u save out of four shillings a week and keep yourself dressed as well? Not you. Of course, if youre a plain woman and can't earn anything more; or if you have a turn for music, or the stage, or newspaper-writing: thats different. But neither Liz nor I had any turn for such things at all: all we had was our appearance and our turn for pleasing men. Do you think we were such fools as to let other people trade in our good looks by employing us as shopgirls, or barmaids, or waitresses, when we could trade in them ourselves and get all the profits instead of starvation wages? Not likely.

VIVIE. You were certainly quite justified--from the business point of view.

MRS WARREN. Yes; or any other point of view. What is any respectable girl brought up to do but to catch some rich man's fancy and get the benefit of his money by marrying him?--as if a marriage ceremony could make any difference in the right or wrong of the thing! Oh, the hypocrisy of the world makes me sick! Liz and I had to work and save and calculate just like other people; elseways we should be as poor as any good-for-nothing drunken waster of a woman that thinks her luck will last for ever. [With great energy] I despise such people: theyve no character; and if theres a thing I hate in a woman, it's want of character.

VIVIE. Come now, mother: frankly! Isn't it part of what you call character in a woman that she should greatly dislike such a way of making money?

MRS WARREN. Why, of course. Everybody dislikes having to work and make money; but they have to do it all the same. I'm sure I've often pitied a poor girl, tired out and in low spirits, having to try to please some man that she doesn't care two straws for--some half-drunken fool that thinks he's making himself agreeable when he's teasing and worrying and disgusting a woman so that hardly any money could pay her for putting up with it. But she has to bear with disagreeables and take the rough with the smooth, just like a nurse in a hospital or anyone else. It's not work that any woman would do for pleasure, goodness knows; though to hear the pious people talk you would suppose it was a bed of roses.

VIVIE. Still, you consider it worth while. It pays.

MRS WARREN. Of course it's worth while to a poor girl, if she can resist temptation and is good-looking and well conducted and sensible. It's far better than any other employment open to her.

I always thought that it oughtn't to be. It *can't* be right, Vivie, that there shouldn't be better opportunities for women. I stick to that: it's wrong. But it's so, right or wrong; and a girl must make the best of it. But of course it's not worth while for a lady. If you took to it youd be a fool; but I should have been a fool if I'd taken to anything else.

VIVIE [more and more deeply moved] Mother: suppose we were both as poor as you were in those wretched old days, are you quite sure that you wouldn't advise me to try the Waterloo bar, or marry a laborer, or even go into the factory?

MRS WARREN [indignantly] Of course not. What sort of mother do you take me for! How could you keep your self-respect in such starvation and slavery? And whats a woman worth? whats life worth? without self-respect! Why am I independent and able to give my daughter a first-rate education, when other women that had just as good opportunities are in the gutter? Because I always knew how to respect myself and control myself. Why is Liz looked up to in a cathedral town? The same reason. Where would we be now if we'd minded the clergyman's foolishness? Scrubbing floors for one and sixpence a day and nothing to look forward to but the workhouse infirmary. Don't you be led astray by people who don't know the world, my girl. The only way for a woman to provide for herself decently is for her to be good to some man that can afford to be good to her. If she's in his own station of life, let her make him marry her; but if she's far beneath him she can't expect it: why should she? it wouldn't be for her own happiness. Ask any lady in London society that has daughters; and she'll tell you the same, except that I tell you straight and she'll tell you crooked. Thats all the difference.

VIVIE [fascinated, gazing at her] My dear mother: you are a wonderful woman: you are stronger than all England. And are you really and truly not one wee bit doubtful--or--or--ashamed?

MRS WARREN. Well, of course, dearie, it's only good manners to be ashamed of it: it's expected from a woman. Women have to pretend to feel a great deal that they don't feel. Liz used to be angry with me for plumping out the truth about it. She used to say that when every woman could learn enough from what was going on in the world before her eyes, there was no need to talk about it to her. But then Liz was such a perfect lady! She had the true instinct of it; while I was always a bit of a vulgarian. I used to be so pleased when you sent me your photos to see that you were growing up like Liz: you've just her ladylike, determined way. But I can't stand saying one thing when everyone knows I mean another. Whats the use in such hypocrisy? If people arrange the world that way for women, theres no good pretending it's arranged the other way. No: I never was a bit ashamed really. I consider I had a right to be proud of how we managed everything so respectably, and never had a word against us, and how the girls were so well taken care of. Some of them did very well: one of them married an ambassador. But of course now I daren't talk about such things: whatever would they think of us! [She yawns]. Oh dear! I do believe I'm getting sleepy after all. [She stretches herself lazily, thoroughly relieved by her explosion, and placidly ready for her night's rest].

VIVIE. I believe it is I who will not be able to sleep now. [She goes to the dresser and lights the candle. Then she extinguishes the lamp, darkening the room a good deal]. Better let in some fresh air before locking up. [She opens the cottage door, and finds that it is broad moonlight]. What a beautiful night! Look! [She draws the curtains of the window. The landscape is seen bathed in the radiance of the harvest moon rising over Blackdown].

MRS WARREN [with a perfunctory glance at the scene] Yes, dear; but take care you don't catch your death of cold from the night air.

VIVIE [contemptuously] Nonsense.

MRS WARREN [querulously] Oh yes: everything I say is nonsense, according to you.

VIVIE [turning to her quickly] No: really that is not so, mother.

You have got completely the better of me tonight, though I intended it to be the other way. Let us be good friends now.

MRS WARREN [shaking her head a little ruefully] So it *has* been the other way. But I suppose I must give in to it. I always got the worst of it from Liz; and now I suppose it'll be the same with you.

VIVIE. Well, never mind. Come: good-night, dear old mother. [She takes her mother in her arms].

MRS WARREN [fondly] I brought you up well, didn't I, dearie?

VIVIE. You did.

MRS WARREN. And youll be good to your poor old mother for it, won't you?

VIVIE. I will, dear. [Kissing her] Good-night.

MRS WARREN [with unction] Blessings on my own dearie darling! a mother's blessing!

[She embraces her daughter protectingly, instinctively looking upward for divine sanction.]

ACT III

[In the Rectory garden next morning, with the sun shining from a cloudless sky. The garden wall has a five-barred wooden gate, wide enough to admit a carriage, in the middle. Beside the gate hangs a bell on a coiled spring, communicating with a pull outside. The carriage drive comes down the middle of the garden and then swerves to its left, where it ends in a little gravelled circus opposite the Rectory porch. Beyond the gate is seen the dusty high road, parallel with the wall, bounded on the farther side by a strip of turf and an unfenced pine wood. On the lawn, between the house and the drive, is a clipped yew tree, with a garden bench in its shade. On the opposite side the garden is shut in by a box hedge; and there is a little sundial on the turf, with an iron chair near it. A little path leads through the box hedge, behind the sundial.]

[Frank, seated on the chair near the sundial, on which he has placed the morning paper, is reading The Standard. His father comes from the house, red-eyed and shivery, and meets Frank's eye with misgiving.]

FRANK [looking at his watch] Half-past eleven. Nice your for a rector to come down to breakfast!

REV. S. Don't mock, Frank: don't mock. I am a little--er--[Shivering]--

FRANK. Off color?

REV. S. [repudiating the expression] No, sir: *unwell* this morning. Where's your mother?

FRANK. Don't be alarmed: she's not here. Gone to town by the 11.13 with Bessie. She left several messages for you. Do you feel equal to receiving them now, or shall I wait til you've breakfasted?

REV. S. I h a v e breakfasted, sir. I am surprised at your mother going to town when we have people staying with us. They'll think it very strange.

FRANK. Possibly she has considered that. At all events, if Crofts is going to stay here, and you are going to sit up every night with him until four, recalling the incidents of your fiery youth, it is clearly my mother's duty, as a prudent housekeeper, to go up to the stores and order a barrel of whisky and a few hundred siphons.

REV. S. I did not observe that Sir George drank excessively.

FRANK. You were not in a condition to, gov'nor.

REV. S. Do you mean to say that *I*--?

FRANK [calmly] I never saw a beneficed clergyman less sober. The anecdotes you told about your past career were so awful that I really don't think Praed would have passed the night under your roof if it hadnt been for the way my mother and he took to one another.

REV. S. Nonsense, sir. I am Sir George Crofts' host. I must talk to him about something; and he has only one subject. Where is Mr Praed now?

FRANK. He is driving my mother and Bessie to the station.

REV. S. Is Crofts up yet?

FRANK. Oh, long ago. He hasn't turned a hair: he's in much better practice than you. Has kept it up ever since, probably. He's taken himself off somewhere to smoke.

[Frank resumes his paper. The parson turns disconsolately towards the gate; then comes back irresolutely.]

REV. S. Er--Frank.

FRANK. Yes.

REV. S. Do you think the Warrens will expect to be asked here after yesterday afternoon?

FRANK. Theyve been asked already.

REV. S. [appalled] What!!!

FRANK. Crofts informed us at breakfast that you told him to bring Mrs Warren and Vivie over here to-day, and to invite them to make this house their home. My mother then found she must go to town by the 11.13 train.

REV. S. [with despairing vehemence] I never gave any such invitation. I never thought of such a thing.

FRANK [compassionately] How do you know, gov'nor, what you said and thought last night?

PRAED [coming in through the hedge] Good morning.

REV. S. Good morning. I must apologize for not having met you at breakfast. I have a touch of--of--

FRANK. Clergyman's sore throat, Praed. Fortunately not chronic.

PRAED [changing the subject] Well I must say your house is in a charming spot here. Really most charming.

REV. S. Yes: it is indeed. Frank will take you for a walk, Mr Praed, if you like. I'll ask you to excuse me: I must take the opportunity to write my sermon while Mrs Gardner is away and you are all amusing yourselves. You won't mind, will you?

PRAED. Certainly not. Don't stand on the slightest ceremony with me.

REV. S. Thank you. I'll--er--er--[He stammers his way to the porch and vanishes into the house].

PRAED. Curious thing it must be writing a sermon every week.

FRANK. Ever so curious, if he did it. He buys em. He's gone for some soda water.

PRAED. My dear boy: I wish you would be more respectful to your father. You know you can be so nice when you like.

FRANK. My dear Praddy: you forget that I have to live with the governor. When two people live together--it don't matter whether theyre father and son or husband and wife or brother and sister--they can't keep up the polite humbug thats so easy for ten minutes on an afternoon call. Now the governor, who unites to many admirable domestic qualities the irresoluteness of a sheep and the pompousness and aggressiveness of a jackass--

PRAED. No, pray, pray, my dear Frank, remember! He is your father.

FRANK. I give him due credit for that. [Rising and flinging down his paper] But just imagine his telling Crofts to bring the Warrens over here! He must have been ever so drunk. You know, my dear Praddy, my mother wouldn't stand Mrs Warren for a moment. Vivie mustn't come here until she's gone back to town.

PRAED. But your mother doesn't know anything about Mrs Warren, does she? [He picks up the paper and sits down to read it].

FRANK. I don't know. Her journey to town looks as if she did. Not that my mother would mind in the ordinary way: she has stuck like a brick to lots of women who had got into trouble. But they were all nice women. Thats what makes the real difference. Mrs Warren, no doubt, has her merits; but she's ever so rowdy; and my mother simply wouldn't put up with her. So--hallo! [This exclamation is provoked by the reappearance of the clergyman, who comes out of the house in haste and dismay].

REV. S. Frank: Mrs Warren and her daughter are coming across the heath with Crofts: I saw them from the study windows. What *am* I to say about your mother?

FRANK. Stick on your hat and go out and say how delighted you are to see them; and that Frank's in the garden; and that mother and Bessie have been called to the bedside of a sick relative, and were ever so sorry they couldn't stop; and that you hope Mrs Warren slept well; and--and--say any blessed thing except the truth, and leave the rest to Providence.

REV. S. But how are we to get rid of them afterwards?

FRANK. Theres no time to think of that now. Here! [He bounds into the house].

REV. S. He's so impetuous. I don't know what to do with him, Mr Praed.

FRANK [returning with a clerical felt hat, which he claps on his father's head]. Now: off with you. [Rushing him through the gate]. Praed and I'll wait here, to give the thing an unpremeditated air. [The clergyman, dazed but obedient, hurries off].

FRANK. We must get the old girl back to town somehow, Praed. Come! Honestly, dear Praddy, do you like seeing them together?

PRAED. Oh, why not?

FRANK [his teeth on edge] Don't it make your flesh creep ever so little? that wicked old devil, up to every villainy under the sun, I'll swear, and Vivie--ugh!

PRAED. Hush, pray. Theyre coming.

[The clergyman and Crofts are seen coming along the road, followed by Mrs Warren and Vivie walking affectionately together.]

FRANK. Look: she actually has her arm round the old woman's waist. It's her right arm: she began it. She's gone sentimental, by God! Ugh! ugh! Now do you feel the creeps? [The clergyman opens the gate: and Mrs Warren and Vivie pass him and stand in the middle of the garden looking at the house. Frank, in an ecstasy of dissimulation, turns gaily to Mrs Warren, exclaiming] Ever so delighted to see you, Mrs Warren. This quiet old rectory garden becomes you perfectly.

MRS WARREN. Well, I never! Did you hear that, George? He says I look well in a quiet old rectory garden.

REV. S. [still holding the gate for Crofts, who loafs through it, heavily bored] You look well everywhere, Mrs Warren.

FRANK. Bravo, gov'nor! Now look here: lets have a treat before lunch. First lets see the church. Everyone has to do that. It's a regular old thirteenth century church, you know: the gov'nor's ever so fond of it, because he got up a restoration fund and had it completely rebuilt six years ago. Praed will be able to shew its points.

PRAED [rising] Certainly, if the restoration has left any to shew.

REV. S. [mooning hospitably at them] I shall be pleased, I'm sure, if Sir George and Mrs Warren really care about it.

MRS WARREN. Oh, come along and get it over.

CROFTS [turning back toward the gate] I've no objection.

REV. S. Not that way. We go through the fields, if you don't mind. Round here. [He leads the way by the little path through the box hedge].

CROFTS. Oh, all right. [He goes with the parson].

[Praed follows with Mrs Warren. Vivie does not stir: she watches them until they have gone, with all the lines of purpose in her face marking it strongly.]

FRANK. Ain't you coming?

VIVIE. No. I want to give you a warning, Frank. You were making fun of my mother just now when you said that about the rectory garden. That is barred in the future. Please treat my mother with as much respect as you treat your own.

FRANK. My dear Viv: she wouldn't appreciate it: the two cases require different treatment. But what on earth has happened to you? Last night we were perfectly agreed as to your mother and her set. This morning I find you attitudinizing sentimentally with your arm around your parent's waist.

VIVIE [flushing] Attitudinizing!

FRANK. That was how it struck me. First time I ever saw you do a second-rate thing.

VIVIE [controlling herself] Yes, Frank: there has been a change: but I don't think it a change for the worse. Yesterday I was a little prig.

FRANK. And today?

VIVIE [wincing; then looking at him steadily] Today I know my mother better than you do.

FRANK. Heaven forbid!

VIVIE. What do you mean?

FRANK. Viv: theres a freemasonry among thoroughly immoral people that you know nothing of. You've too much character. *That's* the bond between your mother and me: that's why I know her better than youll ever know her.

VIVIE. You are wrong: you know nothing about her. If you knew the circumstances against which my mother had to struggle--

FRANK [adroitly finishing the sentence for her] I should know why she is what she is, shouldn't I? What difference would that make? Circumstances or no circumstances, Viv, you won't be able to stand your mother.

VIVIE [very angry] Why not?

FRANK. Because she's an old wretch, Viv. If you ever put your arm around her waist in my presence again, I'll shoot myself there and then as a protest against an exhibition which revolts me.

VIVIE. Must I choose between dropping your acquaintance and dropping my mother's?

FRANK [gracefully] That would put the old lady at ever such a disadvantage. No, Viv: your infatuated little boy will have to stick to you in any case. But he's all the more anxious that you shouldn't make mistakes. It's no use, Viv: your mother's impossible. She may be a good sort; but she's a bad lot, a very bad lot.

VIVIE [hotly] Frank--! [He stands his ground. She turns away and sits down on the bench under the yew tree, struggling to recover her self-command. Then she says] Is she to be deserted by the world because she's what you call a bad lot? Has she no right to live?

FRANK. No fear of that, Viv: *she* won't ever be deserted. [He sits on the bench beside her].

VIVIE. But I am to desert her, I suppose.

FRANK [babyishly, lulling her and making love to her with his voice] Mustn't go live with her. Little family group of mother and daughter wouldn't be a success. Spoil o u r little group.

VIVIE [falling under the spell] What little group?

FRANK. The babes in the wood: Vivie and little Frank. [He nestles against her like a weary child]. Lets go and get covered up with leaves.

VIVIE [rhythmically, rocking him like a nurse] Fast asleep, hand in hand, under the trees.

FRANK. The wise little girl with her silly little boy.

VIVIE. The deal little boy with his dowdy little girl.

FRANK. Ever so peaceful, and relieved from the imbecility of the little boy's father and the questionableness of the little girl's--

VIVIE [smothering the word against her breast] Sh-sh-sh-sh! little girl wants to forget all about her mother. [They are silent for some moments, rocking one another. Then Vivie wakes up with a shock, exclaiming] What a pair of fools we are! Come: sit up. Gracious! your hair. [She smooths it]. I wonder do all grown up people play in that childish way when nobody is looking.

I never did it when I was a child.

FRANK. Neither did I. You are my first playmate. [He catches her hand to kiss it, but checks himself to look around first. Very unexpectedly, he sees Crofts emerging from the box hedge]. Oh damn!

VIVIE. Why damn, dear?

FRANK [whispering] Sh! Here's this brute Crofts. [He sits farther away from her with an unconcerned air].

CROFTS. Could I have a few words with you, Miss Vivie?

VIVIE. Certainly.

CROFTS [to Frank] Youll excuse me, Gardner. Theyre waiting for you in the church, if you don't mind.

FRANK [rising] Anything to oblige you, Crofts--except church. If you should happen to want me, Vivvums, ring the gate bell. [He goes into the house with unruffled suavity].

CROFTS [watching him with a crafty air as he disappears, and speaking to Vivie with an assumption of being on privileged terms with her] Pleasant young fellow that, Miss Vivie. Pity he has no money, isn't it?

VIVIE. Do you think so?

CROFTS. Well, whats he to do? No profession. No property. Whats he good for?

VIVIE. I realize his disadvantages, Sir George.

CROFTS [a little taken aback at being so precisely interpreted] Oh, it's not that. But while we're in this world we're in it; and money's money. [Vivie does not answer]. Nice day, isn't it?

VIVIE [with scarcely veiled contempt for this effort at conversation] Very.

CROFTS [with brutal good humor, as if he liked her pluck] Well thats not what I came to say. [Sitting down beside her] Now listen, Miss Vivie. I'm quite aware that I'm not a young lady's man.

VIVIE. Indeed, Sir George?

CROFTS. No; and to tell you the honest truth I don't want to be either. But when I say a thing I mean it; and when I feel a sentiment I feel it in earnest; and what I value I pay hard money for. Thats the sort of man I am.

VIVIE. It does you great credit, I'm sure.

CROFTS. Oh, I don't mean to praise myself. I have my faults, Heaven knows: no man is more sensible of that than I am. I know I'm not perfect: thats one of the advantages of being a middle-aged man; for I'm not a young man, and I know it. But my code is a simple one, and, I think, a good one. Honor between man and man; fidelity between man and woman; and no can't about this religion or that religion, but an honest belief that things are making for good on the whole.

VIVIE [with biting irony] "A power, not ourselves, that makes for righteousness," eh?

CROFTS [taking her seriously] Oh certainly. Not ourselves, of course. Y o u understand what I mean. Well, now as to practical matters. You may have an idea that I've flung my money about; but I havn't: I'm richer today than when I first came into the property. I've used my knowledge of the world to invest my money in ways that other men have overlooked; and whatever else I may be, I'm a safe man from the money point of view.

VIVIE. It's very kind of you to tell me all this.

CROFTS. Oh well, come, Miss Vivie: you needn't pretend you don't see what I'm driving at. I want to settle down with a Lady Crofts. I suppose you think me very blunt, eh?

VIVIE. Not at all: I am very much obliged to you for being so definite and business-like. I quite appreciate the offer: the money, the position, *Lady Crofts*, and so on. But I think I will say no, if you don't mind, I'd rather not. [She rises, and strolls across to the sundial to get out of his immediate neighborhood].

CROFTS [not at all discouraged, and taking advantage of the additional room left him on the seat to spread himself comfortably, as if a few preliminary refusals were part of the inevitable routine of courtship] I'm in no hurry. It was only just to let you know in case young Gardner should try to trap you. Leave the question open.

VIVIE [sharply] My no is final. I won't go back from it.

[Crofts is not impressed. He grins; leans forward with his elbows on his knees to prod with his stick at some unfortunate insect in the grass; and looks cunningly at her. She turns away impatiently.]

CROFTS. I'm a good deal older than you. Twenty-five years: quarter of a century. I shan't live for ever; and I'll take care that you shall be well off when I'm gone.

VIVIE. I am proof against even that inducement, Sir George. Don't you think youd better take your answer? There is not the slightest chance of my altering it.

CROFTS [rising, after a final slash at a daisy, and coming nearer to her] Well, no matter. I could tell you some things that would change your mind fast enough; but I wont, because I'd rather win you by honest affection. I was a good friend to your mother: ask her whether I wasn't. She'd never have make the money that paid for your education if it hadnt been for my advice and help, not to mention the money I advanced her.

There are not many men who would have stood by her as I have. I put not less than forty thousand pounds into it, from first to last.

VIVIE [staring at him] Do you mean to say that you were my mother's business partner?

CROFTS. Yes. Now just think of all the trouble and the explanations it would save if we were to keep the whole thing in the family, so to speak. Ask your mother whether she'd like to have to explain all her affairs to a perfect stranger.

VIVIE. I see no difficulty, since I understand that the business is wound up, and the money invested.

CROFTS [stopping short, amazed] Wound up! Wind up a business thats paying 35 per cent in the worst years! Not likely. Who told you that?

VIVIE [her color quite gone] Do you mean that it is still--? [She stops abruptly, and puts her hand on the sundial to support herself. Then she gets quickly to the iron chair and sits down].

What business are you talking about?

CROFTS. Well, the fact is it's not what would considered exactly a high-class business in my set--the country set, you know--o u r set it will be if you think better of my offer. Not that theres any mystery about it: don't think that. Of course you know by your mother's being in it that it's perfectly straight and honest. I've known her for many years; and I can say of her that she'd cut off her hands sooner than touch anything that was not what it ought to be. I'll tell you all about it if you like. I don't know whether you've found in travelling how hard it is to find a really comfortable private hotel.

VIVIE [sickened, averting her face] Yes: go on.

CROFTS. Well, thats all it is. Your mother has got a genius for managing such things. We've got two in Brussels, one in Ostend, one in Vienna, and two in Budapest. Of course there are others besides ourselves in it; but we hold most of the capital; and your mother's indispensable as managing director. You've noticed, I daresay, that she travels a good deal. But you see you can't mention such things in society. Once let out the word hotel and everybody thinks you keep a public-house. You wouldn't like people to say that of your mother, would you? Thats why we're so reserved about it. By the way, youll keep it to yourself, won't you? Since it's been a secret so long, it had better remain so.

VIVIE. And this is the business you invite me to join you in?

CROFTS. Oh no. My wife shan't be troubled with business. Youll not be in it more than you've always been.

VIVIE. *I* always been! What do you mean?

CROFTS. Only that you've always lived on it. It paid for your education and the dress you have on your back. Don't turn up your nose at business, Miss Vivie: where would your Newnhams and Girtons be without it?

VIVIE [rising, almost beside herself] Take care. I know what this business is.

CROFTS [starting, with a suppressed oath] Who told you?

VIVIE. Your partner. My mother.

CROFTS [black with rage] The old--

VIVIE. Just so.

[He swallows the epithet and stands for a moment swearing and raging foully to himself. But he knows that his cue is to be sympathetic. He takes refuge in generous indignation.]

CROFTS. She ought to have had more consideration for you. *I'd* never have told you.

VIVIE. I think you would probably have told me when we were married: it would have been a convenient weapon to break me in with.

CROFTS [quite sincerely] I never intended that. On my word as a gentleman I didn't.

[Vivie wonders at him. Her sense of the irony of his protest cools and braces her. She replies with contemptuous self-possession.]

VIVIE. It does not matter. I suppose you understand that when we leave here today our acquaintance ceases.

CROFTS. Why? Is it for helping your mother?

VIVIE. My mother was a very poor woman who had no reasonable choice but to do as she did. You were a rich gentleman; and you did the same for the sake of 35 per cent. You are a pretty common sort of scoundrel, I think. That is my opinion of you.

CROFTS [after a stare: not at all displeased, and much more at his ease on these frank terms than on their former ceremonious ones] Ha! ha! ha! ha! Go it, little missie, go it: it doesn't hurt me and it amuses you. Why the devil shouldn't I invest my money that way? I take the interest on my capital like other people: I hope you don't think I dirty my own hands with the work.

Come! you wouldn't refuse the acquaintance of my mother's cousin the Duke of Belgravia because some of the rents he gets are earned in queer ways. You wouldn't cut the Archbishop of Canterbury, I suppose, because the Ecclesiastical Commissioners have a few publicans and sinners among their tenants. Do you remember your Crofts scholarship at Newnham? Well, that was founded by my brother the M.P. He gets his 22 per cent out of a factory with 600 girls in it, and not one of them getting wages enough to live on. How d'ye suppose they manage when they have no family to fall back on? Ask your mother. And do you expect me to turn my back on 35 per cent when all the rest are pocketing what they can, like sensible men? No such fool! If youre going to pick and choose your acquaintances on moral principles, youd better clear out of this country, unless you want to cut yourself out of all decent society.

VIVIE [conscience stricken] You might go on to point out that I myself never asked where the money I spent came from. I believe I am just as bad as you.

CROFTS [greatly reassured] Of course you are; and a very good thing too! What harm does it do after all? [Rallying her jocularly] So you don't think me such a scoundrel now you come to think it over. Eh?

VIVIE. I have shared profits with you: and I admitted you just now to the familiarity of knowing what I think of you.

CROFTS [with serious friendliness] To be sure you did. You won't find me a bad sort: I don't go in for being superfine intellectually; but Ive plenty of honest human feeling; and the old Crofts breed comes out in a sort of instinctive hatred of anything low, in which I'm sure youll sympathize with me. Believe me, Miss Vivie, the world isn't such a bad place as the croakers make out. As long as you don't fly openly in the face of society, society doesn't ask any inconvenient questions; and it makes precious short work of the cads who do. There are no secrets better kept than the secrets everybody guesses. In the class of people I can introduce you to, no lady or gentleman would so far forget themselves as to discuss my business affairs or your mothers. No man can offer you a safer position.

VIVIE [studying him curiously] I suppose you really think youre getting on famously with me.

CROFTS. Well, I hope I may flatter myself that you think better of me than you did at first.

VIVIE [quietly] I hardly find you worth thinking about at all now. When I think of the society that tolerates you, and the laws that protect you! when I think of how helpless nine out of ten young girls would be in the hands of you and my mother! the unmentionable woman and her capitalist bully--

CROFTS [livid] Damn you!

VIVIE. You need not. I feel among the damned already.

[She raises the latch of the gate to open it and go out. He follows her and puts his hand heavily on the top bar to prevent its opening.]

CROFTS [panting with fury] Do you think I'll put up with this from you, you young devil?

VIVIE [unmoved] Be quiet. Some one will answer the bell. [Without flinching a step she strikes the bell with the back of her hand. It clangs harshly; and he starts back involuntarily. Almost immediately Frank appears at the porch with his rifle].

FRANK [with cheerful politeness] Will you have the rifle, Viv; or shall I operate?

VIVIE. Frank: have you been listening?

FRANK [coming down into the garden] Only for the bell, I assure you; so that you shouldn't have to wait. I think I shewed great insight into your character, Crofts.

CROFTS. For two pins I'd take that gun from you and break it across your head.

FRANK [stalking him cautiously] Pray don't. I'm ever so careless in handling firearms. Sure to be a fatal accident, with a reprimand from the coroner's jury for my negligence.

VIVIE. Put the rifle away, Frank: it's quite unnecessary.

FRANK. Quite right, Viv. Much more sportsmanlike to catch him in a trap. [Crofts, understanding the insult, makes a threatening movement]. Crofts: there are fifteen cartridges in the magazine here; and I am a dead shot at the present distance and at an object of your size.

CROFTS. Oh, you needn't be afraid. I'm not going to touch you.

FRANK. Ever so magnanimous of you under the circumstances! Thank you.

CROFTS. I'll just tell you this before I go. It may interest you, since youre so fond of one another. Allow me, Mister Frank, to introduce you to your half-sister, the eldest daughter of the Reverend Samuel Gardner. Miss Vivie: you half-brother. Good morning! [He goes out through the gate and along the road].

FRANK [after a pause of stupefaction, raising the rifle] Youll testify before the coroner that it's an accident, Viv. [He takes aim at the retreating figure of Crofts. Vivie seizes the muzzle and pulls it round against her breast].

VIVIE. Fire now. You may.

FRANK [dropping his end of the rifle hastily] Stop! take care. [She lets it go. It falls on the turf]. Oh, you've given your little boy such a turn. Suppose it had gone off! ugh! [He sinks on the garden seat, overcome].

VIVIE. Suppose it had: do you think it would not have been a relief to have some sharp physical pain tearing through me?

FRANK [coaxingly] Take it ever so easy, dear Viv. Remember: even if the rifle scared that fellow into telling the truth for the first time in his life, that only makes us the babes in the woods in earnest. [He holds out his arms to her]. Come and be covered up with leaves again.

VIVIE [with a cry of disgust] Ah, not that, not that. You make all my flesh creep.

FRANK. Why, whats the matter?

VIVIE. Goodbye. [She makes for the gate].

FRANK [jumping up] Hallo! Stop! Viv! Viv! [She turns in the gateway] Where are you going to? Where shall we find you?

VIVIE. At Honoria Fraser's chambers, 67 Chancery Lane, for the rest of my life. [She goes off quickly in the opposite direction to that taken by Crofts].

FRANK. But I say--wait--dash it! [He runs after her].

ACT IV

[Honoria Fraser's chambers in Chancery Lane. An office at the top of New Stone Buildings, with a plate-glass window, distempered walls, electric light, and a patent stove. Saturday afternoon. The chimneys of Lincoln's Inn and the western sky beyond are seen through the window. There is a double writing table in the middle of the room, with a cigar box, ash pans, and a portable electric reading lamp almost snowed up in heaps of papers and books. This table has knee holes and chairs right and left and is very untidy. The clerk's desk, closed and tidy, with its high stool, is against the wall, near a door communicating with the inner rooms. In the opposite wall is the door leading to the public corridor. Its upper panel is of opaque glass, lettered in black on the outside, FRASER AND WARREN. A baize screen hides the corner between this door and the window.]

[Frank, in a fashionable light-colored coaching suit, with his stick, gloves, and white hat in his hands, is pacing up and down in the office. Somebody tries the door with a key.]

FRANK [calling] Come in. It's not locked.

s in, in her hat and jacket. She stops and stares at him.]

ıly] What are you doing here?

FRANK. Waiting to see you. I've been here for hours. Is this the way you attend to your business? [He puts his hat and stick on the table, and perches himself with a vault on the clerk's stool, looking at her with every appearance of being in a specially restless, teasing, flippant mood].

VIVIE. I've been away exactly twenty minutes for a cup of tea. [She takes off her hat and jacket and hangs them behind the screen]. How did you get in?

FRANK. The staff had not left when I arrived. He's gone to play cricket on Primrose Hill. Why don't you employ a woman, and give your sex a chance?

VIVIE. What have you come for?

FRANK [springing off the stool and coming close to her] Viv: lets go and enjoy the Saturday half-holiday somewhere, like the staff.

What do you say to Richmond, and then a music hall, and a jolly supper?

VIVIE. Can't afford it. I shall put in another six hours work before I go to bed.

FRANK. Can't afford it, can't we? Aha! Look here. [He takes out a handful of sovereigns and makes them chink]. Gold, Viv: gold!

VIVIE. Where did you get it?

FRANK. Gambling, Viv: gambling. Poker.

VIVIE. Pah! It's meaner than stealing it. No: I'm not coming. [She sits down to work at the table, with her back to the glass door, and begins turning over the papers].

FRANK [remonstrating piteously] But, my dear Viv, I want to talk to you ever so seriously.

VIVIE. Very well: sit down in Honoria's chair and talk here. I like ten minutes chat after tea. [He murmurs]. No use groaning: I'm inexorable. [He takes the opposite seat disconsolately]. Pass that cigar box, will you?

FRANK [pushing the cigar box across] Nasty womanly habit. Nice men don't do it any longer.

VIVIE. Yes: they object to the smell in the office; and we've had to take to cigarets. See! [She opens the box and takes out a cigaret, which she lights. She offers him one; but he shakes his head with a wry face. She settles herself comfortably in her chair, smoking]. Go ahead.

FRANK. Well, I want to know what you've done--what arrangements you've made.

VIVIE. Everything was settled twenty minutes after I arrived here. Honoria has found the business too much for her this year; and she was on the point of sending for me and proposing a partnership when I walked in and told her I hadn't a farthing in the world. So I installed myself and packed her off for a fortnight's holiday. What happened at Haslemere when I left?

FRANK. Nothing at all. I said youd gone to town on particular business.

VIVIE. Well?

FRANK. Well, either they were too flabbergasted to say anything, or else Crofts had prepared your mother. Anyhow, she didn't say anything; and Crofts didn't say anything; and Praddy only stared. After tea they got up and went; and I've not seen them since.

VIVIE [nodding placidly with one eye on a wreath of smoke] Thats all right.

FRANK [looking round disparagingly] Do you intend to stick in this confounded place?

VIVIE [blowing the wreath decisively away, and sitting straight up] Yes. These two days have given me back all my strength and self-possession. I will never take a holiday again as long as I live.

FRANK [with a very wry face] Mps! You look quite happy. And as hard as nails.

VIVIE [grimly] Well for me that I am!

FRANK [rising] Look here, Viv: we must have an explanation. We parted the other day under a complete misunderstanding. [He sits on the table, close to her].

VIVIE [putting away the cigaret] Well: clear it up.

FRANK. You remember what Crofts said.

VIVIE. Yes.

FRANK. That revelation was supposed to bring about a complete change in the nature of our feeling for one another. It placed us on the footing of brother and sister.

VIVIE. Yes.

FRANK. Have you ever had a brother?

VIVIE. No.

FRANK. Then you don't know what being brother and sister feels like? Now I have lots of sisters; and the fraternal feeling is quite familiar to me. I assure you my feeling for you is not the least in the world like it. The girls will go *their* way; I will go mine; and we shan't care if we never see one another again. Thats brother and sister. But as to you, I can't be easy if I have to pass a week without seeing you. Thats not brother and sister. Its exactly what I felt an hour before Crofts made his revelation. In short, dear Viv, it's love's young dream.

VIVIE [bitingly] The same feeling, Frank, that brought your father to my mother's feet. Is that it?

FRANK [so revolted that he slips off the table for a moment] I very strongly object, Viv, to have my feelings compared to any which the Reverend Samuel is capable of harboring; and I object still more to a comparison of you to your mother. [Resuming his perch] Besides, I don't believe the story. I have taxed my father with it, and obtained from him what I consider tantamount to a denial.

VIVIE. What did he say?

FRANK. He said he was sure there must be some mistake.

VIVIE. Do you believe him?

FRANK. I am prepared to take his word against Crofts'.

VIVIE. Does it make any difference? I mean in your imagination or conscience; for of course it makes no real difference.

FRANK [shaking his head] None whatever to *me*.

VIVIE. Nor to me.

FRANK [staring] But this is ever so surprising! [He goes back to his chair]. I thought our whole relations were altered in your imagination and conscience, as you put it, the moment those words were out of that brute's muzzle.

VIVIE. No: it was not that. I didn't believe him. I only wish I could.

FRANK. Eh?

VIVIE. I think brother and sister would be a very suitable relation for us.

FRANK. You really mean that?

VIVIE. Yes. It's the only relation I care for, even if we could afford any other. I mean that.

FRANK [raising his eyebrows like one on whom a new light has dawned, and rising with quite an effusion of chivalrous sentiment] My dear Viv: why didn't you say so before? I am ever so sorry for persecuting you. I understand, of course.

VIVIE [puzzled] Understand what?

FRANK. Oh, I'm not a fool in the ordinary sense: only in the Scriptural sense of doing all the things the wise man declared to be folly, after trying them himself on the most extensive scale. I see I am no longer Vivvums's little boy. Don't be alarmed: I shall never call you Vivvums again--at least unless you get tired of your new little boy, whoever he may be.

VIVIE. My new little boy!

FRANK [with conviction] Must be a new little boy. Always happens that way. No other way, in fact.

VIVIE. None that you know of, fortunately for you.

[Someone knocks at the door.]

FRANK. My curse upon yon caller, whoe'er he be!

VIVIE. It's Praed. He's going to Italy and wants to say goodbye. I asked him to call this afternoon. Go and let him in.

FRANK. We can continue our conversation after his departure for Italy. I'll stay him out. [He goes to the door and opens it]. How are you, Praddy? Delighted to see you. Come in.

[Praed, dressed for travelling, comes in, in high spirits.]

PRAED. How do you do, Miss Warren? [She presses his hand cordially, though a certain sentimentality in his high spirits jars upon her]. I start in an hour from Holborn Viaduct. I wish I could persuade you to try Italy.

VIVIE. What for?

PRAED. Why, to saturate yourself with beauty and romance, of course.

[Vivie, with a shudder, turns her chair to the table, as if the work waiting for her there were a support to her. Praed sits opposite to her. Frank places a chair near Vivie, and drops lazily and carelessly into it, talking at her over his shoulder.]

FRANK. No use, Praddy. Viv is a little Philistine. She is indifferent to *my* romance, and insensible to *my* beauty.

VIVIE. Mr Praed: once for all, there is no beauty and no romance in life for me. Life is what it is; and I am prepared to take it as it is.

PRAED [enthusiastically] You will not say that if you come with me to Verona and on to Venice. You will cry with delight at living in such a beautiful world.

FRANK. This is most eloquent, Praddy. Keep it up.

PRAED. Oh, I assure you *I* have cried--I shall cry again, I hope--at fifty! At your age, Miss Warren, you would not need to go so far as Verona. Your spirits would absolutely fly up at the mere sight of Ostend. You would be charmed with the gaiety, the vivacity, the happy air of Brussels.

VIVIE [springing up with an exclamation of loathing] Agh!

PRAED [rising] Whats the matter?

FRANK [rising] Hallo, Viv!

VIVIE [to Praed, with deep reproach] Can you find no better example of your beauty and romance than Brussels to talk to me about?

PRAED [puzzled] Of course it's very different from Verona. I don't suggest for a moment that--

VIVIE [bitterly] Probably the beauty and romance come to much the same in both places.

PRAED [completely sobered and much concerned] My dear Miss Warren: I--[looking enquiringly at Frank] Is anything the matter?

FRANK. She thinks your enthusiasm frivolous, Praddy. She's had ever such a serious call.

VIVIE [sharply] Hold your tongue, Frank. Don't be silly.

FRANK [sitting down] Do you call this good manners, Praed?

PRAED [anxious and considerate] Shall I take him away, Miss Warren? I feel sure we have disturbed you at your work.

VIVIE. Sit down: I'm not ready to go back to work yet. [Praed sits]. You both think I have an attack of nerves. Not a bit of it. But there are two subjects I want dropped, if you don't mind.

One of them [to Frank] is love's young dream in any shape or form: the other [to Praed] is the romance and beauty of life, especially Ostend and the gaiety of Brussels. You are welcome to any illusions you may have left on these subjects: I have none. If we three are to remain friends, I must be treated as a woman of business, permanently single [to Frank] and permanently unromantic [to Praed].

FRANK. I also shall remain permanently single until you change your mind. Praddy: change the subject. Be eloquent about something else.

PRAED [diffidently] I'm afraid theres nothing else in the world that I *can* talk about. The Gospel of Art is the only one I can preach. I know Miss Warren is a great devotee of the Gospel of Getting On; but we can't discuss that without hurting your feelings, Frank, since you are determined not to get on.

FRANK. Oh, don't mind my feelings. Give me some improving advice by all means: it does me ever so much good. Have another try to make a successful man of me, Viv. Come: lets have it all: energy, thrift, foresight, self-respect, character. Don't you hate people who have no character, Viv?

VIVIE [wincing] Oh, stop, stop. Let us have no more of that horrible cant. Mr Praed: if there are really only those two gospels in the world, we had better all kill ourselves; for the same taint is in both, through and through.

FRANK [looking critically at her] There is a touch of poetry about you today, Viv, which has hitherto been lacking.

PRAED [remonstrating] My dear Frank: aren't you a little unsympathetic?

VIVIE [merciless to herself] No: it's good for me. It keeps me from being sentimental.

FRANK [bantering her] Checks your strong natural propensity that way, don't it?

VIVIE [almost hysterically] Oh yes: go on: don't spare me. I was sentimental for one moment in my life--beautifully sentimental--by moonlight; and now--

FRANK [quickly] I say, Viv: take care. Don't give yourself away.

VIVIE. Oh, do you think Mr Praed does not know all about my mother? [Turning on Praed] You had better have told me that morning, Mr Praed. You are very old fashioned in your delicacies, after all.

PRAED. Surely it is you who are a little old fashioned in your prejudices, Miss Warren. I feel bound to tell you, speaking as an artist, and believing that the most intimate human relationships are far beyond and above the scope of the law, that though I know that your mother is an unmarried woman, I do not respect her the less on that account. I respect her more.

FRANK [airily] Hear! hear!

VIVIE [staring at him] Is that *all* you know?

PRAED. Certainly that is all.

VIVIE. Then you neither of you know anything. Your guesses are innocence itself compared with the truth.

PRAED [rising, startled and indignant, and preserving his politeness with an effort] I hope not. [More emphatically] I hope not, Miss Warren.

FRANK [whistles] Whew!

VIVIE. You are not making it easy for me to tell you, Mr Praed.

PRAED [his chivalry drooping before their conviction] If there is anything worse--that is, anything else--are you sure you are right to tell us, Miss Warren?

VIVIE. I am sure that if I had the courage I should spend the rest of my life in telling everybody--stamping and branding it into them until they all felt their part in its abomination as I feel mine. There is nothing I despise more than the wicked convention that protects these things by forbidding a woman to mention them. And yet I can't tell you. The two infamous words that describe what my mother is are ringing in my ears and struggling on my tongue; but I can't utter them: the shame of them is too horrible for me. [She buries her face in her hands. The two men, astonished, stare at one another and then at her. She raises her head again desperately and snatches a sheet of paper and a pen]. Here: let me draft you a prospectus.

FRANK. Oh, she's mad. Do you hear, Viv? mad. Come! pull yourself together.

VIVIE. You shall see. [She writes]. "Paid up capital: not less than forty thousand pounds standing in the name of Sir George Crofts, Baronet, the chief shareholder. Premises at Brussels, Ostend, Vienna, and Budapest. Managing director: Mrs Warren"; and now don't let us forget h e r qualifications: the two words. [She writes the words and pushes the paper to them]. There! Oh no: don't read it: don't! [She snatches it back and tears it to pieces; then seizes her head in her hands and hides her face on the table].

[Frank, who has watched the writing over her shoulder, and opened his eyes very widely at it, takes a card from his pocket; scribbles the two words on it; and silently hands it to Praed, who reads it with amazement, and hides it hastily in his pocket.]

FRANK [whispering tenderly] Viv, dear: thats all right. I read what you wrote: so did Praddy. We understand. And we remain, as this leaves us at present, yours ever so devotedly.

PRAED. We do indeed, Miss Warren. I declare you are the most splendidly courageous woman I ever met.

[This sentimental compliment braces Vivie. She throws it away from her with an impatient shake, and forces herself to stand up, though not without some support from the table.]

FRANK. Don't stir, Viv, if you don't want to. Take it easy.

VIVIE. Thank you. You an always depend on me for two things: not to cry and not to faint. [She moves a few steps towards the door of the inner room, and stops close to Praed to say] I shall need much more courage than that when I tell my mother that we have come to a parting of the ways. Now I must go into the next room for a moment to make myself neat again, if you don't mind.

PRAED. Shall we go away?

VIVIE. No: I'll be back presently. Only for a moment. [She goes into the other room, Praed opening the door for her].

PRAED. What an amazing revelation! I'm extremely disappointed in Crofts: I am indeed.

FRANK. I'm not in the least. I feel he's perfectly accounted for at last. But what a facer for me, Praddy! I can't marry her now.

PRAED [sternly] Frank! [The two look at one another, Frank unruffled, Praed deeply indignant]. Let me tell you, Gardner, that if you desert her now you will behave very despicably.

FRANK. Good old Praddy! Ever chivalrous! But you mistake: it's not the moral aspect of the case: it's the money aspect. I really can't bring myself to touch the old woman's money now.

PRAED. And was that what you were going to marry on?

FRANK. What else? *I* havn't any money, nor the smallest turn for making it. If I married Viv now she would have to support me; and I should cost her more than I am worth.

PRAED. But surely a clever bright fellow like you can make something by your own brains.

FRANK. Oh yes, a little. [He takes out his money again]. I made all that yesterday in an hour and a half. But I made it in a highly speculative business. No, dear Praddy: even if Bessie and Georgina marry millionaires and the governor dies after cutting them off with a shilling, I shall have only four hundred a year. And he won't die until he's three score and ten: he hasn't originality enough. I shall be on short allowance for the next twenty years. No short allowance for Viv, if I can help it. I withdraw gracefully and leave the field to the gilded youth of England. So that settled. I shan't worry her about it: I'll just send her a little note after we're gone. She'll understand.

PRAED [grasping his hand] Good fellow, Frank! I heartily beg your pardon. But must you never see her again?

FRANK. Never see her again! Hang it all, be reasonable. I shall come along as often as possible, and be her brother. I can *not* understand the absurd consequences you romantic people expect from the most ordinary transactions. [A knock at the door]. I wonder who this is. Would you mind opening the door? If it's a client it will look more respectable than if I appeared.

PRAED. Certainly. [He goes to the door and opens it. Frank sits down in Vivie's chair to scribble a note]. My dear Kitty: come in: come in.

[Mrs Warren comes in, looking apprehensively around for Vivie. She has done her best to make herself matronly and dignified. The brilliant hat is replaced by a sober bonnet, and the gay blouse covered by a costly black silk mantle. She is pitiably anxious and ill at ease: evidently panic-stricken.]

MRS WARREN [to Frank] What! Y o u r e here, are you?

FRANK [turning in his chair from his writing, but not rising] Here, and charmed to see you. You come like a breath of spring.

MRS WARREN. Oh, get out with your nonsense. [In a low voice] Where's Vivie?

[Frank points expressively to the door of the inner room, but says nothing.]

MRS WARREN [sitting down suddenly and almost beginning to cry] Praddy: won't she see me, don't you think?

PRAED. My dear Kitty: don't distress yourself. Why should she not?

MRS WARREN. Oh, you never can see why not: youre too innocent. Mr Frank: did she say anything to you?

FRANK [folding his note] She *must* see you, if [very expressively] you wait til she comes in.

MRS WARREN [frightened] Why shouldn't I wait?

[Frank looks quizzically at her; puts his note carefully on the ink-bottle, so that Vivie cannot fail to find it when next she dips her pen; then rises and devotes his attention entirely to her.]

FRANK. My dear Mrs Warren: suppose you were a sparrow--ever so tiny and pretty a sparrow hopping in the roadway--and you saw a steam roller coming in your direction, would you wait for it?

MRS WARREN. Oh, don't bother me with your sparrows. What did she run away from Haslemere like that for?

FRANK. I'm afraid she'll tell you if you rashly await her return.

MRS WARREN. Do you want me to go away?

FRANK. No: I always want you to stay. But I *advise* you to go away.

MRS WARREN. What! And never see her again!

FRANK. Precisely.

MRS WARREN [crying again] Praddy: don't let him be cruel to me. [She hastily checks her tears and wipes her eyes]. She'll be so angry if she sees I've been crying.

FRANK [with a touch of real compassion in his airy tenderness] You know that Praddy is the soul of kindness, Mrs Warren. Praddy: what do you say? Go or stay?

PRAED [to Mrs Warren] I really should be very sorry to cause you unnecessary pain; but I think perhaps you had better not wait. The fact is--[Vivie is heard at the inner door].

FRANK. Sh! Too late. She's coming.

MRS WARREN. Don't tell her I was crying. [Vivie comes in. She stops gravely on seeing Mrs Warren, who greets her with hysterical cheerfulness]. Well, dearie. So here you are at last.

VIVIE. I am glad you have come: I want to speak to you. You said you were going, Frank, I think.

FRANK. Yes. Will you come with me, Mrs Warren? What do you say to a trip to Richmond, and the theatre in the evening? There is safety in Richmond. No steam roller there.

VIVIE. Nonsense, Frank. My mother will stay here.

MRS WARREN [scared] I don't know: perhaps I'd better go. We're disturbing you at your work.

VIVIE [with quiet decision] Mr Praed: please take Frank away. Sit down, mother. [Mrs Warren obeys helplessly].

PRAED. Come, Frank. Goodbye, Miss Vivie.

VIVIE [shaking hands] Goodbye. A pleasant trip.

PRAED. Thank you: thank you. I hope so.

FRANK [to Mrs Warren] Goodbye: youd ever so much better have taken my advice. [He shakes hands with her. Then airily to Vivie] Byebye, Viv.

VIVIE. Goodbye. [He goes out gaily without shaking hands with her].

PRAED [sadly] Goodbye, Kitty.

MRS WARREN [snivelling]--oobye!

[Praed goes. Vivie, composed and extremely grave, sits down in Honoria's chair, and waits for her mother to speak. Mrs Warren, dreading a pause, loses no time in beginning.]

MRS WARREN. Well, Vivie, what did you go away like that for without saying a word to me! How could you do such a thing! And what have you done to poor George? I wanted him to come with me; but he shuffled out of it. I could see that he was quite afraid of you. Only fancy: he wanted me not to come. As if [trembling] I should be afraid of you, dearie. [Vivie's gravity deepens]. But of course I told him it was all settled and comfortable between us, and that we were on the best of terms. [She breaks down]. Vivie: whats the meaning of this? [She produces a commercial envelope, and fumbles at the enclosure with trembling fingers]. I got it from the bank this morning.

VIVIE. It is my month's allowance. They sent it to me as usual the other day. I simply sent it back to be placed to your credit, and asked them to send you the lodgment receipt. In future I shall support myself.

MRS WARREN [not daring to understand] Wasn't it enough? Why didn't you tell me? [With a cunning gleam in her eye] I'll double it: I was intending to double it. Only let me know how much you want.

VIVIE. You know very well that that has nothing to do with it. From this time I go my own way in my own business and among my own friends. And you will go yours. [She rises]. Goodbye.

MRS WARREN [rising, appalled] Goodbye?

VIVIE. Yes: goodbye. Come: don't let us make a useless scene: you understand perfectly well. Sir George Crofts has told me the whole business.

MRS WARREN [angrily] Silly old--[She swallows an epithet, and then turns white at the narrowness of her escape from uttering it].

VIVIE. Just so.

MRS WARREN. He ought to have his tongue cut out. But I thought it was ended: you said you didn't mind.

VIVIE [steadfastly] Excuse me: I *do* mind.

MRS WARREN. But I explained--

VIVIE. You explained how it came about. You did not tell me that it is still going on [She sits].

[Mrs Warren, silenced for a moment, looks forlornly at Vivie, who waits, secretly hoping that the combat is over. But the cunning expression comes back into Mrs Warren's face; and she bends across the table, sly and urgent, half whispering.]

MRS WARREN. Vivie: do you know how rich I am?

VIVIE. I have no doubt you are very rich.

MRS WARREN. But you don't know all that that means; youre too young. It means a new dress every day; it means theatres and balls every night; it means having the pick of all the gentlemen in Europe at your feet; it means a lovely house and plenty of servants; it means the choicest of eating and drinking; it means everything you like, everything you want, everything you can think of. And what are you here? A mere drudge, toiling and moiling early and late for your bare living and two cheap dresses a year. Think over it. [Soothingly] Youre shocked, I know. I can enter into your feelings; and I think they do you credit; but trust me, nobody will blame you: you may take my word for that. I know what young girls are; and I know youll think better of it when you've turned it over in your mind.

VIVIE. So that's how it is done, is it? You must have said all that to many a woman, to have it so pat.

MRS WARREN [passionately] What harm am I asking you to do? [Vivie turns away contemptuously. Mrs Warren continues desperately] Vivie: listen to me: you don't understand: you were taught wrong on purpose: you don't know what the world is really like.

VIVIE [arrested] Taught wrong on purpose! What do you mean?

MRS WARREN. I mean that youre throwing away all your chances for nothing. You think that people are what they pretend to be: that the way you were taught at school and college to think right and proper is the way things really are. But it's not: it's all only a pretence, to keep the cowardly slavish common run of people quiet. Do you want to find that out, like other women, at forty, when you've thrown yourself away and lost your chances; or won't you take it in good time now from your own mother, that loves you and swears to you that it's truth: gospel truth? [Urgently] Vivie: the big people, the clever people, the managing people, all know it. They do as I do, and think what I think. I know plenty of them. I know them to speak to, to introduce you to, to make friends of for you. I don't mean anything wrong: thats what you don't understand: your head is full of ignorant ideas about me. What do the people that taught you know about life or about people like me? When did they ever meet me, or speak to me, or let anyone tell them about me? the fools! Would they ever have done anything for you if I hadn't paid them? Havn't I told you that I want you to be respectable? Havn't I brought you up to be respectable? And how can you keep it up without my money and my influence and Lizzie's friends? Can't you see that youre cutting your own throat as well as breaking my heart in turning your back on me?

VIVIE. I recognize the Crofts philosophy of life, mother. I heard it all from him that day at the Gardners'.

MRS WARREN. You think I want to force that played-out old sot on you! I don't, Vivie: on my oath I don't.

VIVIE. It would not matter if you did: you would not succeed. [Mrs Warren winces, deeply hurt by the implied indifference towards her affectionate intention. Vivie, neither understanding this nor concerning herself about it, goes on calmly] Mother: you don't at all know the sort of person I am. I don't object to Crofts more than to any other coarsely built man of his class. To tell you the truth, I rather admire him for being strongminded enough to enjoy himself in his own way and make plenty of money instead of living the usual shooting, hunting, dining-out, tailoring, loafing life of his set merely because all the rest do it. And I'm perfectly aware that if I'd been in the same circumstances as my aunt Liz, I'd have done exactly what she did.

I don't think I'm more prejudiced or straitlaced than you: I think I'm less. I'm certain I'm less sentimental. I know very well that fashionable morality is all a pretence, and that if I took your money and devoted the rest of my life to spending it fashionably, I might be as worthless and vicious as the silliest woman could possibly be without having a word said to me about it. But I don't want to be worthless. I shouldn't enjoy trotting about the park to advertize my dressmaker and carriage builder, or being bored at the opera to shew off a shopwindowful of diamonds.

MRS WARREN [bewildered] But--

VIVIE. Wait a moment: I've not done. Tell me why you continue your business now that you are independent of it. Your sister, you told me, has left all that behind her. Why don't you do the same?

MRS WARREN. Oh, it's all very easy for Liz: she likes good society, and has the air of being a lady. Imagine *me* in a cathedral town! Why, the very rooks in the trees would find me out even if I could stand the dulness of it. I must have work and excitement, or I should go melancholy mad. And what else is there for me to do? The life suits me: I'm fit for it and not for anything else. If I didn't do it somebody else would; so I don't do any real harm by it. And then it brings in money; and I like making money. No: it's no use: I can't give it up--not for anybody. But what need you know about it? I'll never mention it. I'll keep Crofts away. I'll not trouble you much: you see I have to be constantly running about from one place to another. Youll be quit of me altogether when I die.

VIVIE. No: I am my mother's daughter. I am like you: I must have work, and must make more money than I spend. But my work is not your work, and my way is not your way. We must part. It will not make much difference to us: instead of meeting one another for perhaps a few months in twenty years, we shall never meet: thats all.

MRS WARREN [her voice stifled in tears] Vivie: I meant to have been more with you: I did indeed.

VIVIE. It's no use, mother: I am not to be changed by a few cheap tears and entreaties any more than you are, I daresay.

MRS WARREN [wildly] Oh, you call a mother's tears cheap.

VIVIE. They cost you nothing; and you ask me to give you the peace and quietness of my whole life in exchange for them. What use would my company be to you if you could get it? What have we two in common that could make either of us happy together?

MRS WARREN [lapsing recklessly into her dialect] We're mother and daughter. I want my daughter. I've a right to you. Who is to care for me when I'm old? Plenty of girls have taken to me like daughters and cried at leaving me; but I let them all go because I had you to look forward to. I kept myself lonely for you. You've no right to turn on me now and refuse to do your duty as a daughter.

VIVIE [jarred and antagonized by the echo of the slums in her mother's voice] My duty as a daughter! I thought we should come to that presently. Now once for all, mother, you want a daughter and Frank wants a wife. I don't want a mother; and I don't want a husband. I have spared neither Frank nor myself in sending him about his business. Do you think I will spare you?

MRS WARREN [violently] Oh, I know the sort you are: no mercy for yourself or anyone else. _I_ know. My experience has done that for me anyhow: I can tell the pious, canting, hard, selfish woman when I meet her. Well, keep yourself to yourself: _I_ don't want you. But listen to this. Do you know what I would do with you if you were a baby again? aye, as sure as there's a Heaven above us.

VIVIE. Strangle me, perhaps.

MRS WARREN. No: I'd bring you up to be a real daughter to me, and not what you are now, with your pride and your prejudices and the college education you stole from me: yes, stole: deny it if you can: what was it but stealing? I'd bring you up in my own house, I would.

VIVIE [quietly] In one of your own houses.

MRS WARREN [screaming] Listen to her! listen to how she spits on her mother's grey hairs! Oh, may you live to have your own daughter tear and trample on you as you have trampled on me. And you will: you will. No woman ever had luck with a mother's curse on her.

VIVIE. I wish you wouldn't rant, mother. It only hardens me. Come: I suppose I am the only young woman you ever had in your power that you did good to. Don't spoil it all now.

MRS WARREN. Yes, Heaven forgive me, it's true; and you are the only one that ever turned on me. Oh, the injustice of it! the injustice! the injustice! I always wanted to be a good woman. I tried honest work; and I was slave-driven until I cursed the day I ever heard of honest work. I was a good mother; and because I made my daughter a good woman she turns me out as if I were a leper. Oh, if I only had my life to live over again! I'd talk to that lying clergyman in the school. From this time forth, so help me Heaven in my last hour, I'll do wrong and nothing but wrong. And I'll prosper on it.

VIVIE. Yes: it's better to choose your line and go through with it. If I had been you, mother, I might have done as you did; but I should not have lived one life and believed in another. You are a conventional woman at heart. That is why I am bidding you goodbye now. I am right, am I not?

MRS WARREN [taken aback] Right to throw away all my money!

VIVIE. No: right to get rid of you? I should be a fool not to. Isn't that so?

MRS WARREN [sulkily] Oh well, yes, if you come to that, I suppose you are. But Lord help the world if everybody took to doing the right thing! And now I'd better go than stay where I'm not wanted. [She turns to the door].

VIVIE [kindly] Won't you shake hands?

MRS WARREN [after looking at her fiercely for a moment with a savage impulse to strike her] No, thank you. Goodbye.

VIVIE [matter-of-factly] Goodbye. [Mrs Warren goes out, slamming the door behind her. The strain on Vivie's face relaxes; her grave expression breaks up into one of joyous content; her breath goes out in a half sob, half laugh of intense relief. She goes buoyantly to her place at the writing table; pushes the electric lamp out of the way; pulls over a great sheaf of papers; and is in the act of dipping her pen in the ink when she finds Frank's note. She opens it unconcernedly and reads it quickly, giving a little laugh at some quaint turn of expression in it]. And goodbye, Frank. [She tears the note up and tosses the pieces into the wastepaper basket without a second thought. Then she goes at her work with a plunge, and soon becomes absorbed in its figures].

Printed in Great Britain
by Amazon

39361258R00046